Light, Life, and

by W. R. Ing

INTRODUCTION

Sect. 1. THE PRECURSORS OF THE GERMAN MYSTICS

TO most English readers the "Imitation of Christ" is the representative of mediaeval German mysticism. In reality, however, this beautiful little treatise belongs to a period when that movement had nearly spent itself. Thomas a Kempis, as Dr. Bigg has said,[1] was only a semi-mystic. He tones down the most characteristic doctrines of Eckhart, who is the great original thinker of the German mystical school, and seems in some ways to revert to an earlier type of devotional literature. The "Imitation" may perhaps be described as an idealised picture of monastic piety, drawn at a time when the life of the cloister no longer filled a place of unchallenged usefulness in the social order of Europe. To find German mysticism at its strongest we must go back a full hundred years, and to understand its growth we must retrace our steps as far as the great awakening of the thirteenth century--the age of chivalry in religion--the age of St. Louis, of Francis and Dominic, of Bonaventura and Thomas Aquinas. It was a vast revival, bearing fruit in a new ardour of pity and charity, as well as in a healthy freedom of thought. The Church, in recognising the new charitable orders of Francis and Dominic, and the Christianised Aristotelianism of the schoolmen, retained the loyalty and profited by the zeal of the more sober reformers, but was unable to prevent the diffusion of an independent critical spirit, in part provoked and justified by real abuses. Discontent was aroused, not only by the worldiness of the hierarchy, whose greed and luxurious living were felt to be scandalous, but by the widespread economic distress which prevailed over Western Europe at this period. The crusades periodically swept off a large proportion of the able-bodied men, of whom the majority never returned to their homes, and this helped to swell the number of indigent women, who, having no male protectors, were obliged to beg their bread. The better class of these female mendicants soon formed themselves into uncloistered charitable Orders, who were not forbidden to marry, and who devoted themselves chiefly to the care of the sick. These Beguines and the corresponding male associations of Beghards became very numerous in Germany. Their religious views were of a definite type. Theirs was an intensely inward religion, based on the longing of the soul for immediate access to God. The more educated among them tended to embrace a vague idealistic Pantheism. Mechthild of Magdeburg (1212-1277), prophetess, poetess, Church reformer, quietist, was the ablest of the Beguines.

Her writings prove to us that the technical terminology of German mysticism was in use before Eckhart,[2] and also that the followers of what the "Theologia Germanica" calls the False Light, who aspired to absorption in the Godhead, and despised the imitation of the incarnate Christ, were already throwing discredit on the movement. Mechthild's independence, and her unsparing denunciations of corruption in high places, brought her into conflict with the secular clergy. They tried to burn her books--those religious love songs which had already endeared her to German popular sentiment. It was then that she seemed to hear a voice saying to her:

Lieb' meine, betrŸbe dich nicht zu sehr,

Die Wahrheit mag niemand verbrennen!

The rulers of the Church, unhappily, were not content with burning books. Their hostility towards the unrecognised Orders became more and more pronounced: the Beghards and Beguines were harried and persecuted till most of them were driven to join the Franciscans or Dominicans, carrying with them into those Orders the ferment of their speculative mysticism. The more stubborn "Brethren and Sisters of the Free Spirit" were burned in batches at Cologne and elsewhere. Their fate in those times did not excite much pity, for many of the victims were idle vagabonds of dissolute character, and the general public probably thought that the licensed begging friars were enough of a nuisance without the addition of these free lances.

The heretical mystical sects of the thirteenth century are very interesting as illustrating the chief dangers of mysticism. Some of these sectaries were Socialists or Communists of an extreme kind; others were Rationalists, who taught that Jesus Christ was the son of Joseph and a sinner like other men; others were Puritans, who said that Church music was "nothing but a hellish noise" (nihil nisi clamor inferni), and that the Pope was the magna meretrix of the Apocalypse. The majority were Anti-Sacramentalists and Determinists; and some were openly Antinomian, teaching that those who are led by the Spirit can do no wrong. The followers of Amalric of Bena[3] believed that the Holy Ghost had chosen their sect in which to become incarnate; His presence among them was a continual guarantee of sanctity and happiness. The "spiritual Franciscans" had dreams of a more apocalyptic kind. They adopted the idea of an "eternal Gospel," as expounded by Joachim of Floris, and believed that the "third kingdom," that of the Spirit, was about to begin among themselves. It was to abolish the secular Church and to inaugurate the reign of true Christianity--i.e. "poverty" and asceticism.

Such are some of the results of what our eighteenth-century ancestors knew and dreaded as "Enthusiasm"--that ferment of the spirit which in certain epochs spreads from soul to soul like an epidemic, breaking all the fetters of authority, despising tradition and rejecting discipline in its eagerness to get rid of formalism and unreality; a lawless, turbulent, unmanageable spirit, in which, notwithstanding, is a potentiality for good far higher than any to which the lukewarm "religion of all sensible men" can ever attain. For mysticism is the raw material of all religion; and it is easier to discipline the enthusiast than to breathe enthusiasm into the disciplinarian.

Meanwhile, the Church looked with favour upon the orthodox mystical school, of which Richard and Hugo of St. Victor, Bonaventura, and Albertus Magnus were among the greatest names. These men were working out in their own fashion the psychology of the contemplative life, showing how we may ascend through "cogitation, meditation, and speculation" to "contemplation," and how we may pass successively through jubilus, ebrietas spiritus, spiritualis jucunditas, and liquefactio, till we attain raptus or ecstasy. The writings of the scholastic mystics are so overweighted with this pseudo-science, with its wire-drawn distinctions and meaningless classifications, that very few readers have now the patience to dig out their numerous beauties. They are, however, still the classics of mystical theology in the Roman Church, so far as that science has not degenerated into mere miracle-mongering.

Sect. 2. MEISTER ECKHART

It was in 1260, when Mechthild of Magdeburg was at the height of her activity, that Meister Eckhart, next to Plotinus the greatest philosopher-mystic, was born at Hocheim in Thuringia. It seems that his family was in a good position, but nothing is known of his early years. He entered the Dominican Order as a youth, perhaps at sixteen, the earliest age at which novices were admitted into that Order. The course of instruction among the Dominicans was as follows:--After two years, during which the novice laid the foundations of a good general education, he devoted the next two years to grammar, rhetoric, and dialectic, and then the same amount of time to what was called the

Quadrivium, which consisted of "arithmetic, mathematics, astronomy, and music." Theology, the queen of the sciences, occupied three years; and at the end of the course, at the age of twenty-five, the brothers were ordained priests. We find Eckhart, towards the end of the century, Prior of Erfurt and Vicar of Thuringia, then Lector Biblicus at Paris, then Provincial Prior of Saxony. In 1307 the master of the Order appointed him Vicar-General for Bohemia, and in 1311 he returned to Paris. We find him next preaching busily at Strassburg,[4] and after a few more years, at Cologne, where the persecution of the Brethren of the Free Spirit was just then at its height. At Strassburg there were no less than seven convents of Dominican nuns, for since 1267 the Order had resumed the supervision of female convents, which it had renounced a short time after its foundation. Many of Eckhart's discourses were addressed to these congregations of devout women, who indeed were to a large extent the backbone of the mystical movement, and it is impossible not to see that the devotional treatises of the school are strongly coloured by feminine sentiment. A curious poem, written by a Dominican nun of this period, celebrates the merits of three preachers, the third of whom is a Master Eckhart, "who speaks to us about Nothingness. He who understands him not, in him has never shone the light divine." These nuns seem to have been fed with the strong meat of Eckhart's mystical philosophy; in the more popular sermons he tried to be intelligible to all. It was not very long after he took up his residence at Cologne that he was himself attacked for heresy. In 1327 he read before his own Order a retractation of "any errors which might be found" (si quid errorum repertum fuerit) in his writings, but withdrew nothing that he had actually said, and protested that he believed himself to be orthodox. He died a few months later, and it was not till 1329 that a Papal bull was issued, enumerating seventeen heretical and eleven objectionable doctrines in his writings.

This bull is interesting as showing what were the points in Eckhart's teaching which in the fourteenth century were considered dangerous. They also indicate very accurately what are the real errors into which speculative mysticism is liable to fall, and how thinkers of this school may most plausibly be misrepresented by those who differ from them. After expressing his sorrow that "a certain Teuton named Ekardus, doctor, ut fertur, sacrae paginae, has wished to know more than he should," and has sown tares and thistles and other weeds in the field of the Church, the Pope specifies the following erroneous statements as appearing in Eckhart's writings[5]:--1. "God created the world as soon as God was. 2. In every work, bad as well as good, the glory of God is equally manifested. 3. A man who prays for any particular thing prays for an evil and prays ill, for he prays for the negation of good and the negation of God, and that God may be denied to him.[6] 4. God is honoured in those who have renounced everything, even holiness and the kingdom of heaven. 5. We are transformed totally into God, even as in the Sacrament the bread is converted into the Body of Christ. Unum, non simile. 6. Whatever God the Father gave to His only-begotten Son in His human nature, He has given it all to me. 7. Whatever the Holy Scripture says about Christ is verified in every good and godlike man. 8. External action is not, properly speaking, good nor divine; God, properly speaking, only works in us internal actions. 9. God is one, in every way and according to every reason, so that it is not possible to find any plurality in Him, either in the intellect or outside it; for he who sees two, or sees any distinction, does not see God; for God is one, outside number and above number, for one cannot be put with anything else, but follows it; therefore in God Himself no distinction can be or be understood. 10. All the creatures are absolutely nothing: I say not that they are small or something, but that they are absolutely nothing." All these statements are declared to have been found in his writings. It is also "objected against the said Ekardus" that he taught the following two articles in these words:--1. "There is something in the soul, which is uncreated and uncreatable: if the whole soul were such, it would be uncreated and uncreatable: and this is the intelligence.[7] 2. God is not good or better or best: I speak ill when I call God good; it is as if I called white black."[8] The bull declares all the propositions above quoted to be heretical, with the exception of the three which I have numbered 8-10, and these "have an ill sound" and are "very rash," even if they might be so supplemented and explained as to bear an orthodox sense.

This condemnation led to a long neglect of Eckhart's writings. He was almost forgotten till Franz Pfeiffer in 1857 collected and edited his scattered treatises and endeavoured to distinguish those which were genuine from those which were spurious. Since Pfeiffer's edition fresh discoveries have been made, notably in 1880, when Denifle found at Erfurt several important fragments in Latin, which in his opinion show a closer dependence on the scholastic theology, and particularly on St Thomas Aquinas, than Protestant scholars, such as Preger, had been willing to allow. But the attempt to prove Eckhart a mere scholastic is a failure; the audacities of his German discourses cannot be explained as an accommodation to the tastes of a peculiar audience. For good or evil Eckhart is an original and independent thinker, whose theology is confined by no trammels of authority.

Sect. 3. ECKHART'S RELIGIOUS PHILOSOPHY

The Godhead, according to Eckhart, is the universal and eternal Unity comprehending and transcending all diversity. "The Divine nature is Rest," he says in one of the German discourses; and in the Latin fragments we find: "God rests in Himself, and makes all things rest in Him." The three Persons of the Trinity, however, are not mere modes or accidents,[9] but represent a real distinction within the Godhead. God is unchangeable, and at the same time an "everlasting process." The creatures are "absolutely nothing"; but at the same time "God without them would not be God," for God is love, and must objectify Himself; He is goodness, and must impart Himself. As the picture in the mind of the painter, as the poem in the mind of the poet, so was all creation in the mind of God from all eternity, in uncreated simplicity. The ideal world was not created in time; "the Father spake Himself and all the creatures in His Son"; "they exist in the eternal Now"[10]--"a becoming without a becoming, change without change." "The Word of God the Father is the substance of all that exists, the life of all that lives, the principle and cause of life." Of creation he says: "We must not falsely imagine that God stood waiting for something to happen, that He might create the world. For so soon as He was God, so soon as He begat His coeternal and coequal Son, He created the world." So Spinoza says: "God has always been before the creatures, without even existing before them. He precedes them not by an interval of time, but by a fixed eternity." This is not the same as saying that the world of sense had no beginning; it is possible that Eckhart did not mean to go further than the orthodox scholastic mystic, Albertus Magnus, who says: "God created things from eternity, but the things were not created from eternity." St Augustine (Conf. xi. 30) bids objectors to "understand that there can be no time without creatures, and cease to talk nonsense." Eckhart also tries to distinguish between the "interior" and the "exterior" action of God. God, he says, is in all things, not as Nature, not as Person, but as Being. He is everywhere, undivided; yet the creatures participate in Him according to their measure.[11] The three Persons of the Trinity have impressed their image upon the creatures, yet it is only their "nothingness" that keeps them separate creatures. Most of this comes from the Neoplatonists, and much of it through the pseudo-Dionysius the Areopagite, a Platonising Christian of the fifth century, whose writings were believed in the

Middle Ages to proceed from St Paul's Athenian convert. It would, however, be easy to find parallels in St Augustine's writings to most of the phases quoted in this paragraph. The practical consequences will be considered presently.

The creatures are a way from God; they are also a way to Him. "In Christ," he says, "all the creatures are one man, and that man is God." Grace, which is a real self-unfolding of God in the soul, can make us "what God is by Nature"--one of Eckhart's audacious phrases, which are not really so unorthodox as they sound. The following prayer, which appears in one of his discourses, may perhaps be defended as asking no more than our Lord prayed for (John xvii.) for His disciples, but it lays him open to the charge, which the Pope's bull did not fail to urge against him, that he made the servant equal to his Lord. "Grant that I, by Thy grace, may be united to Thy Nature, as Thy Son is eternally one in Thy Nature, and that grace may become my nature."

The ethical aim is to be rid of "creatureliness," and so to be united to God. In Eckhart's system, as in that of Plotinus, speculation is never divorced from ethics. On our side the process is a negative one. All our knowledge must be reduced to not-knowledge; our reason and will, as well as our lower faculties, must transcend themselves, must die to live. We must detach ourselves absolutely "even from God," he says. This state of spiritual nudity he calls "poverty." Then, when our house is empty of all else, God can dwell there: "He begets His Son in us." This last phrase has always been a favourite with the mystics. St Paul uses very similar language, and the Epistle to Diognetus, written in the second century, speaks of Christ as, "being ever born anew in the hearts of the saints." Very characteristic, too, is the doctrine that complete detachment from the creatures is the way to union with God. Jacob Böhme has arrived independently at the same conclusion as Eckhart. "The scholar said to his master: How may I come to the supersensual life, that I may see God and hear Him speak? The master said: When thou canst throw thyself but for a moment into that place where no creature dwelleth, then thou hearest what God speaketh. The scholar asked: Is that near or far off? The master replied: It is in thee, and if thou canst for a while cease from all thy thinking and willing, thou shalt hear unspeakable words of God. The scholar said: How can I hear, when I stand still from thinking and willing? The master answered: When thou standest still from the thinking and willing of self, the eternal hearing, seeing, and speaking will be revealed to thee, and so God heareth and seeth through thee."

In St Thomas Aquinas it is "the will enlightened by reason" which unites us to God. But there are two sorts of reason. The passive reason is the faculty which rises through discursive thinking to knowledge. The active reason is a much higher faculty, which exists by participation in the divine mind, "as the air is light by participation in the sunshine." When this active reason is regarded as the standard of moral action, it is called by Aquinas synteresis.[12] Eckhart was at first content with this teaching of St Thomas, whom he always cites with great reverence; but the whole tendency of his thinking was to leave the unprofitable classification of faculties in which the Victorine School almost revelled, and to concentrate his attention on the union of the soul with God. And therefore in his more developed teaching,[13] the "spark" which is the point of contact between the soul and its Maker is something higher than the faculties, being "uncreated." He seems to waver about identifying the "spark" with the "active reason," but inclines on the whole to regard it as something even higher still. "There is something in the soul," he says, "which is so akin to God that it is one with Him and not merely united with Him." And again: "There is a force in the soul; and not only a force, but something more, a being; and not only a being, but something more; it is so pure and high and noble in itself that no creature can come there, and God alone can dwelt there. Yea, verily, and even God cannot come there with a form; He can only come with His simple divine nature." And in the startling passage often quoted against him, a passage which illustrates admirably his affinity to one side of Hegelianism, we read: "The eye with which I see God is the same eye with which He sees me. Mine eye and God's eye are one eye and one sight and one knowledge and one love."

I do not defend these passages as orthodox; but before exclaiming "rank Pantheism!" we ought to recollect that for Eckhart the being of God is quite different from His personality. Eckhart never taught that the Persons of the Holy Trinity become, after the mystical Union, the "Form" of the human soul. It is the impersonal light of the divine nature which transforms our nature; human personality is neither lost nor converted into divine personality. Moreover, the divine spark at the centre of the soul is not the soul nor the personality. "The soul," he says in one place, using a figure which recurs in the "Theologia Germanica," "has two faces. One is turned towards this world and towards the body, the other towards God." The complete dominion of the "spark" over the soul is an unrealised ideal.[14]

The truth which he values is that, as Mr Upton[15] has well expressed it, "there is a certain self-revelation of the eternal and infinite One to the finite soul, and therefore an indestructible basis for religious ideas and beliefs as distinguished from what is called scientific knowledge. . . . This immanent universal principle does not pertain to, and is not the property of any individual mind, but belongs to that uncreated and eternal nature of God which lies deeper than all those differences which separate individual minds from each other, and is indeed that incarnation of the Eternal, who though He is present in every finite thing, is still not broken up into individualities, but remains one and the same eternal substance, one and the same unifying principle, immanently and indivisibly present in every one of the countless plurality of finite individuals." It might further be urged that neither God nor man can be understood in independence of each other. A recent writer on ethics,[16] not too well disposed towards Christianity, is, I think, right in saying: "To the popular mind, which assumes God and man to be two different realities, each given in independence of the other, . . . the identification of man's love of God with God's love of Himself has always been a paradox and a stumbling-block. But it is not too much to say that until it has been seen to be no paradox, but a simple and fundamental truth, the masterpieces of the world's religious literature must remain a sealed book to us."

Eckhart certainly believed himself to have escaped the pitfall of Pantheism; but he often expressed himself in such an unguarded way that the charge may be brought against him with some show of reason.

Love, Eckhart teaches, is the principle of all virtues; it is God Himself. Next to it in dignity comes humility. The beauty of the soul, he says in the true Platonic vein, is to be well ordered, with the higher faculties above the lower, each in its proper place. The will should be supreme over the understanding, the understanding over the senses. Whatever we will earnestly, that we have, and no one can hinder us from attaining that detachment from the creatures in which our blessedness consists.

Evil, from the highest standpoint, is only a means for realising the eternal aim of God in creation; all will ultimately be overruled for good. Nevertheless, we can frustrate the good will of God towards us, and it is this, and not the thought of any insult against Himself, that makes God grieve for our sins. It would not be worth while to give any more quotations on this subject, for Eckhart is not more successful than other philosophers in propounding a consistent and intelligible theory of the place of evil in the universe.

Eckhart is well aware of the two chief pitfalls into which the mystic is liable to fall--dreamy inactivity and Antinomianism. The sects of the Free Spirit seem to have afforded a good object-lesson in both these errors, as some of the Gnostic sects did in the second century. Eckhart's teaching here is sound and good. Freedom from law, he says, belongs only to the "spark," not to the faculties of the soul, and no man can live always on the highest plane. Contemplation is, in a sense, a means to activity; works of charity are its proper fruit. "If a man were in an ecstasy like that of St Paul, when he was caught up into the third heaven, and knew of a poor man who needed his help, he ought to leave his ecstasy and help the needy." Suso[17] tells us how God punished him for disregarding this duty. True contemplation considers Reality (or Being) in its manifestations as well as in its origin. If this is remembered, there need be no conflict between social morality and the inner life. Eckhart recognises[18] that it is a harder and a nobler task to preserve detachment in a crowd than in a cell; the little daily sacrifices of family life are often a greater trial than self-imposed mortifications. "We need not destroy any little good in ourselves for the sake of a better, but we should strive to grasp every truth in its highest meaning, for no one good contradicts another." "Love God, and do as you like, say the Free Spirits. Yes; but as long as you like anything contrary to God's will, you do not love Him."

There is much more of the same kind in Eckhart's sermons--as good and sensible doctrine as one could find anywhere. But what was the practical effect of his teaching as a whole? It is generally the case that the really weak points of any religious movement are exposed with a cruel logicality most exasperating to the leaders by the second generation of its adherents. The dangerous side of the Eckhartian mysticism is painfully exhibited in the life of his spiritual daughter, "Schwester Katrei," the saint of the later Beguines. Katrei is a rather shadowy person; but for our present purpose it does not much matter whether the story of her life has been embroidered or not. Her memory was revered for such sayings and doings as these which follow. On one occasion she exclaimed: "Congratulate me; I have become God!" and on another she declared that "not even the desire of heaven should tempt a good man towards activity." It was her ambition to forget who were her parents, to be indifferent whether she received absolution and partook of the Holy Communion or not; and she finally realised her ambition by falling into a cataleptic state in which she was supposed to be dead, and was carried out for burial. Her confessor, perceiving that she was not really dead, awoke her: "Art thou satisfied?" "I am satisfied at last," said Katrei: she was now "dead all through," as she wished to be.

Are we to conclude that the logical outcome of mysticism is this strange reproduction, in Teutonic Europe, of Indian Yogism? Many who have studied the subject have satisfied themselves that Schwester Katrei is the truly consistent mystic. They have come to the conclusion that the real attraction of mysticism is a pining for deliverance from this fretful, anxious, exacting, individual life, and a yearning for absorption into the great Abyss where all distinctions are merged in the Infinite. According to this view, mysticism in its purest form should be studied in the ancient religious literature of India, which teaches us how all this world of colour and diversity, of sharp outlines and conflicting forces, may be lost and swallowed up in the "white radiance," or black darkness (it does not really matter which we call it) of an empty Infinite.

The present writer is convinced that this is not the truth about mysticism. Eckhart may have encouraged Schwester Katrei in her attempt to substitute the living death of the blank trance for the dying life of Christian charity; but none the less she caricatured and stultified his teaching. And I think it is possible to lay our finger on the place where she and so many others went wrong. The aspiration of mysticism is to find the unity which underlies all diversity, or, in religious language, to see God face to face. From the Many to the One is always the path of the mystic. Plotinus, the father of all mystical philosophy in Europe (unless, as he himself would have wished, we give that honour to Plato), mapped out the upward road as follows:--At the bottom of the hill is the sphere of the "merely many"--of material objects viewed in disconnection, dull, and spiritless. This is a world which has no real existence; it may best be called "not-being" ("ein lauteres Nichts," as Eckhart says), and as the indeterminate, it can only be apprehended by a corresponding indeterminateness in the soul. The soul, however, always adds some form and determination to the abstract formlessness of the "merely many." Next, we rise to, or project for ourselves, the world of "the one and the many." This is the sphere in which our consciousness normally moves. We are conscious of an overruling Mind, but the creatures still seem external to and partially independent of it. Such is the temporal order as we know it. Above this is the intelligible world, the eternal order, "the one-many," das ewige Nu, the world in which God's will is done perfectly and all reflects the divine mind. Highest of all is "the One," the, Absolute, the Godhead, of whom nothing can be predicated, because He is above all distinctions. This Neoplatonic Absolute is the Godhead of whom Eckhart says: "God never looked upon deed," and of whom Angelus Silesius sings:

"Und sieh, er ist nicht Wille, Er ist ein' ewige Stille."

Plotinus taught that the One, being superessential, can only be apprehended in ecstasy, when thought, which still distinguishes itself from its object, is transcended, and knower and known become one. As Tennyson's Ancient Sage says:

"If thou would'st hear the Nameless, and descend Into the Temple-cave of thine own self, There, brooding by the central altar, thou May'st haply learn the Nameless hath a voice, By which thou wilt abide, if thou be wise; For knowledge is the swallow on the lake, That sees and stirs the surface-shadow there But never yet hath dipt into the Abysm."

In the same way Eckhart taught that no creature can apprehend the Godhead, and, therefore, that the spark in the centre of the soul (this doctrine, too, is found in Plotinus) must be verily divine. The logic of the theory is inexorable. If only like can know like, we cannot know God except by a faculty which is itself divine. The real question is whether God, as an object of knowledge and worship for finite beings, is the absolute Godhead, who transcends all distinctions. The mediaeval mystics held that this "flight of the alone to the alone," as Plotinus calls it, is possible to men, and that in it consists our highest blessedness. They were attracted towards this view by several influences. First, there was the tradition of Dionysius, to whom (e.g.) the author of the "Theologia Germanica" appeals as an authority for the possibility of "beholding the hidden things of God by utter abandonment of thyself, and of entering into union with Him who is above all existence, and all knowledge." Secondly, there was what a modern writer has called "the attraction of the Abyss," the longing which some persons feel very strongly to merge their individuality in a larger and better whole, to get rid not only of selfishness but of self for ever. "Leave nothing of myself in me," is Crashaw's prayer in his wonderful poem on St Teresa. Thirdly, we may mention the awe and respect long paid to ecstatic trances, the pathological nature of which was not understood. The blank trance was a real experience; and as it could be induced by a long course of ascetical exercises and fervid devotions, it was naturally regarded as the crowning reward of sanctity on earth. Nor would it be at all safe to reject the evidence, which is very copious,[19] that the "dreamy state" may issue in permanent spiritual gain. The methodical cultivation of it, which is at the bottom of most of the strange austerities of the ascetics, was not only (though it was partly) practised in the hope of enjoying those spiritual raptures which are described as being far more intense than any pleasures of sense[20]: it was the hope of stirring to its depths the subconscious mind and permeating the whole with the hidden energy of the divine Spirit that led to the desire for visions and trances. Lastly, I think we must give a place to the intellectual attraction of an uncompromising monistic theory of the universe. Spiritualistic monism, when it is consistent with itself, will always lean to semi-pantheistic mysticism rather than to such a compromise with pluralism as Lotze and his numerous followers in this country imagine to be possible.

But it is possible to go a long way with the mystics and yet to maintain that under no conditions whatever can a finite being escape from the limitations of his finitude and see God or the world or himself "with the same eye with which God sees" all things. The old Hebrew belief, that to see the face of God is death, expresses the truth under a mythical form. That the human mind, while still "in the body pent," may obtain glimpses of the eternal order, and enjoy foretastes of the bliss of heaven, is a belief which I, at least, see no reason to reject. It involves no rash presumption, and is not contrary to what may be readily believed about the state of immortal spirits passing through a mortal life. But the explanation of the blank trance as a temporary transit into the Absolute must be set down as a pure delusion. It involves a conception of the divine "Rest" which in his best moments Eckhart himself repudiates. "The Rest of the Godhead," he says, "is not in that He is the source of being, but in that He is the consummation of all being." This profound saying expresses the truth, which he seems often to forget, that the world-process must have a real value in God's sight--that it is not a mere polarisation of the white radiance of eternity broken up by the imperfection of our vision. Whatever theories we may hold about Absolute Being, or an Absolute that is above Being, we must make room for the Will, and for Time, which is the "form" of the will, and for the creatures who inhabit time and space, as having for us the value of reality. Nor shall we, if we are to escape scepticism, be willing to admit that these appearances have no sure relation to ultimate reality. We must not try to uncreate the world in order to find God. We were created out of nothing, but we cannot return to nothing, to find our Creator there. The still, small voice is best listened for amid the discordant harmony of life and death.

The search for God is no exception to the mysterious law of human nature, that we cannot get anything worth having--neither holiness nor happiness nor wisdom--by trying for it directly. It must be given us through something else. The recluse who lives like Parnell's "Hermit":

"Prayer all his business, all his pleasure praise,"

is not only a poor sort of saint, but he will offer a poor sort of prayers and praises. He will miss real holiness for the same reason that makes the pleasure-seeker miss real happiness. We must lose ourselves in some worthy interest in order to find again both a better self and an object higher than that which we sought. This the German mystics in a sense knew well. There is a noble sentence of Suso to the effect that "he who realises the inward in the outward, to him the inward becomes more inward than to him who only recognises the inward in the inward." Moreover, the recognition that "God manifests Himself and worketh more in one creature than another" ("Theologia Germanica"), involves a denial of the nihilistic view that all the creatures are "ein lauteres Nichts."[21] It would be easy to find such passages in all the fourteenth-century mystics, but it cannot be denied that on the whole their religion is too self-centred. There are not many maxims so fundamentally wrong-headed and un-Christian as Suso's advice to "live as if you were the only person in the world."[22] The life of the cloistered saint may be abundantly justified--for the spiritual activity of some of them has been of far greater service to mankind than the fussy benevolence of many "practical" busybodies--but the idea of social service, whether in the school of Martha or of Mary, ought surely never to be absent. The image of Christ as the Lover of the individual soul rather than as the Bridegroom of the Church was too dear to these lonely men and women. Unconsciously, they looked to their personal devotions to compensate them for the human loves which they had forsworn. The raptures of Divine Love, which they regarded as signal favours bestowed upon them, were not very wholesome in themselves, and diverted their thoughts from the needs of their fellow-men. They also led to most painful reactions, in which the poor contemplative believed himself abandoned by God and became a pray to terrible depression and melancholy. These fits of wretchedness came indeed to be recognised as God's punishment for selfishness in devotion and for too great desire for the sweetness of communing with God, and so arose the doctrine of "disinterested love," which was more and more emphasised in the later mysticism, especially by the French Quietists.

I have spoken quite candidly of the defects of Eckhart's mystical Christianity. As a religious philosophy it does not keep clear of the fallacy that an ascent though the unreal can lead to reality. "To suppose, as the mystic does, that the finite search has of itself no Being at all, is illusory, is Maya, is itself nothing, this is also to deprive the Absolute of even its poor value as a contrasting goal. For a goal that is a goal of no real process has as little value as it has content."[23] But, as Prof. Royce says, mysticism furnishes us with the means of correcting itself. It supplies an obvious reductio ad absurdum of the theory with which it set out, that "Immediacy is the one test of reality," and is itself forced to give the world of diversity a real value as manifesting in different degrees the nature of God. Those who are acquainted with the sacred books of the East will recognise that here is the decisive departure from real Pantheism. And it may be fairly claimed for the German mystics that though their speculative teaching sometimes seems to echo too ominously the apathetic detachment of the Indian sage, their lives and example, and their practical exhortations, preached a truer and a larger philosophy. Eckhart, as we have seen, was a busy preacher as well as a keen student, and some of the younger members of his school were even more occupied in pastoral work. If the tree is to be judged by its fruits, mysticism can give a very good account of itself to the Marthas as well as the Marys of this world.

Sect. 4. THE GERMAN MYSTICS AS GUIDES TO HOLINESS

THIS little volume is a contribution to a "Library of Devotion," and in the body of the work the reader will be seldom troubled by any abstruse philosophising. I have thought it necessary to give, in this Introduction, a short account of Eckhart's system, but the extracts which follow are taken mainly from his successors, in whom the speculative tendency is weaker and less original, while the religious element is stronger and more attractive. It is, after all, as guides to holiness that these mystics are chiefly important to us. This side of their life's work can never be out of date, for the deeper currents of human nature change but little; the language of the heart is readily understood everywhere and at all times. The differences between Catholic and Protestant are hardly felt in the keen air of these high summits. It was Luther himself who discovered the "Theologia Germanica" and said of it that, "next to the Bible and St Augustine, no book hath ever come into my hands whence I have learnt or would wish to learn more of what God and Christ and man and all things are. I thank God that I have heard and found my God in the German tongue, as I have not yet found Him in Latin, Greek, or Hebrew." The theology of these mystics takes us straight back to the Johannine doctrine of Christ as the all-pervading Word of God, by whom all things were made and in whom all things hold together. He is not far from any one of us if we will but seek Him where He is to be found--in the innermost sanctuary of our personal life. In personal religion this means that no part of revelation is to be regarded as past, isolated, or external. "We should mark and know of a very truth," says the author of the "Theologia Germanica," "that all manner of virtue and goodness, and even the eternal Good which is God Himself, can never make a man virtuous, good, or happy, so long as it is outside the soul." In the same spirit Jacob Bšhme, 250 years later, says: "If the sacrifice of Christ is to avail for me, it must be wrought in me." Or, as his English admirer, William Law, puts it: "Christ given for us is neither more nor less than Christ given into us. He is in no other sense our full, perfect, and sufficient Atonement than as His nature and spirit are born and formed in us." The whole process of redemption must in a sense be reenacted in the inner life of every Christian. And as Christ emptied Himself for our sakes, so must we empty ourselves of all self-seeking. "When the creature claimeth for its own anything good, such as life, knowledge, or power, and in short whatever we commonly call good, as if it were that, or possessed that--it goeth astray." Sin is nothing else but self-assertion, self-will. "Be assured," says the "Theologia Germanica," "that he who helpeth a man to his own will, helpeth him to the worst that he can." He, therefore, who is "simply and wholly bereft of self" is delivered from sin, and God alone reigns in his inmost soul. Concerning the highest part or faculty of the soul, the author of this little treatise follows Eckhart, but cautiously. "The True Light," he says, "is that eternal Light which is God; or else it is a created light, but yet Divine, which is called grace." In either case, "where God dwells in a godly man, in such a man somewhat appertaineth to God which is His own, and belongs to Him only and not to the creature." This doctrine of divine immanence, for which there is ample warrant in the New Testament, is the real kernel of German mysticism. It is a doctrine which, when rightly used, may make this world a foretaste of heaven, but alas! the "False Light" is always trying to counterfeit the true. In the imitation of the suffering life of Christ lies the only means of escaping the deceptions of the Evil One. "The False Light dreameth itself to be God, and sinless"; but "none is without sin; if any is without consciousness of sin, he must be either Christ or the Evil Spirit."

Very characteristic is the teaching of all these writers about rewards and punishments. Without in any way impugning the Church doctrine of future retribution, they yet agree with Benjamin Whichcote, the Cambridge Platonist, that "heaven is first a temper, then a place"; while of hell there is much to recall the noble sentence of Juliana of Norwich, the fourteenth-century visionary, "to me was showed no harder hell than sin." "Nothing burneth in hell but self-will," is a saying in the "Theologia Germanica."[24] They insist that the difference between heaven and hell is not that one is a place of enjoyment, the other of torment; it is that in the one we are with Christ, in the other without Him. "The Christlike life is not chosen," to quote the "Theologia Germanica" once more, "in order to serve any end, or to get anything by it, but for love of its nobleness, and because God loveth and esteemeth it so highly. He who doth not take it up for love, hath none of it at all; he may dream indeed that he hath put it on, but he is deceived. Christ did not lead such a life as this for the sake of reward, but out of love, and love maketh such a life light, and taketh away all its hardships, so that it becometh sweet and is gladly endured." The truly religious man is always more concerned about what God will do in him than what He will do to him; in his intense desire for the purification of his motives he almost wishes that heaven and hell were blotted out, that he might serve God for Himself alone.

Sect. 5. WRITERS OF THE SCHOOL OF ECKHART--TAULER

Such are the main characteristics of the religious teachings which we find in the German mystics. Among the successors of Eckhart, from whose writings the following extracts are taken, the most notable names are those of Tauler, Suso, and Ruysbroek. From Tauler I have taken very little, because a volume of selections from his sermons has already appeared in this series.[25] Accordingly, it will only be necessary to mention a very few facts about his life.

John Tauler was born at Strassburg about 1300, and studied at the Dominican convents of Strassburg and Cologne. At both places he doubtless heard the sermons of Eckhart. In 1329 the great interdict began at Strassburg, and was stoutly resisted by many of the clergy. It is a disputed point whether Tauler himself obeyed the Papal decree or not. His uneventful life, which was devoted to study, preaching, and pastoral work, came to an end in 1361. Like Eckhart, he had a favourite "spiritual daughter," Margaret Ebner, who won a great reputation as a visionary.

Sect. 6. SUSO

Henry Suso was born in 1295 and died in 1365. His autobiography was published not long before his death. He is the poet of the band. The romance of saintship is depicted by him with a strange vividness which alternately attracts and repels, or even disgusts, the modern reader. The whole-hearted devotion of the "Servitor" to the "Divine Wisdom," the tender beauty of the visions and conversations, and the occasional na•vet?of the narrative, which shows that the saint remained very human throughout, make Suso's books delightful reading; but the accounts of the horrible macerations to which he subjected himself for many years shock our moral sense almost as much as our sensibilities; we do not now believe that God takes pleasure in sufferings inflicted in His honour. Moreover, the erotic symbolism of the visions is occasionally unpleasant: we are no longer in the company of such sane and healthy people as Eckhart and Tauler. The half-sensuous pleasure of ecstasy was evidently a temptation to Suso, and the violent alternations of rapture and misery which he experienced suggest a neurotic and ill-balanced temperament.[26]

On this subject--the pathological side of mysticism--a few remarks will not be out of place, for there has been much discussion of it lately. A great deal of nonsense has been written on the connexion between religion and neuroticism. To quote Professor James' vigorous protest, "medical materialism finishes up St Paul by calling his vision on the road to Damascus a discharging lesion of the occipital cortex, he being an epileptic. It snuffs out St Teresa as an hysteric, St Francis of Assisi as an hereditary degenerate. George Fox's discontent with the shams of his age, and his pining for spiritual veracity, it treats as a symptom of a disordered colon. Carlyle's organ-tones of misery it accounts for by a gastro-duodenal catarrh. All such mental over-tensions, it says, are, when you come to the bottom of the matter, mere affairs of diathesis (auto-intoxications most probably), due to the perverted action of various glands which physiology will yet discover."[27] Now, even if it were true that most religious geniuses, like most other geniuses, have been "psychopaths" of one kind or another, this fact in no way disposes of the value of their intuitions and experiences. Nearly all the great benefactors of humanity have been persons of one-sided, and therefore ill-balanced, characters. Even Maudsley admits that "Nature may find an incomplete mind a more suitable instrument for a particular purpose. It is the work that is done, and the quality in the worker by which it is done, that is alone of moment; and it may be no great matter from a cosmical standpoint, if in other qualities of character he (the genius) was singularly defective."[28] Except in the character of our Lord Himself, there are visible imperfections in the record of every great saint; but that is no reason for allowing such traces of human infirmity to discredit what is pure and good in their work. More particularly, it would be a great pity to let our minds dwell on the favourite materialistic theory that saintliness, especially as cultivated and venerated by Catholicism, has its basis in "perverted sexuality." There is enough plausibility in the theory to make it mischievous. The allegorical interpretation of the Book of Canticles was in truth the source of, or at least the model for, a vast amount of unwholesome and repulsive pietism. Not a word need be said for such a paltry narrative of endearments and sickly compliments as the "Revelations of the Nun Gertrude," in the thirteenth century. Nor are we concerned to deny that the artificially induced ecstasy, which is desired on account of the intense pleasure which is said to accompany it, nearly always contains elements the recognition of which would shock and distress the contemplatives themselves.[29] There are, however, other elements, of a less insidious kind, which make the ecstatic trance seem desirable. These are, according to Professor Leuba, the calming of the restless intellect by the concentration of the mind on one object; the longing for a support and comfort more perfect than man can give; and, thirdly, the consecration and strengthening of the will, which is often a permanent effect of the trance. These are legitimate objects of desire, and in many of the mystics they are much more prominent than any tendencies which might be considered morbid. As regards the larger question, about the alleged pathological character of all distinctively religious exaltation, I believe that no greater mistake could be made than to suppose that the religious life flourishes best in unnatural circumstances. Religion, from a biological standpoint, I take to be the expression of the racial will to live; its function (from this point of view) is the preservation and development of humanity on the highest possible level. If this is true, a simple, healthy, natural life must be the most favourable for religious excellence--and this I believe to be the case. Poor Suso certainly did not lead a healthy or natural life. But in his case, though the suppressed natural instincts obviously overflow into the religious consciousness and in part determine the forms which his devotion assumes, we can never forget that we are in the company of a poet and a saint who will lift us, if we can follow him, into a very high region of the spiritual life, an altitude which he has himself climbed with bleeding feet.

The simple confidence which at the end of the dialogue he expresses in the value of his work is, I think, amply justified. "Whoever will read these writings of mine in a right spirit, can hardly fail to be stirred to the depths of his soul, either to fervent love, or to new light, or to hunger and thirst for God, or to hatred and loathing for his sins, or to that spiritual aspiration by which the soul is renewed in grace."

Sect. 7. RUYSBROEK

[Note: the Ruysbroek selection has not been reproduced in this electronic edition. An electronic text of a larger collection of Ruysbroek's works may be available.]

Sect. 8. THEOLOGIA GERMANICA

The "Theologia Germanica," an isolated treatise of no great length by an unknown author, was written towards the end of the fourteenth century by one of the Gottesfreunde, a widespread association of pious souls in Germany. He is said to have been "a priest and warden of the house of the Teutonic Order at Frankfort." His book is both the latest and one of the most important productions of the German mystical school founded by Eckhart. The author is a deeply religious philosopher, as much interested in speculative mysticism as Eckhart himself, but as thoroughly penetrated with devout feeling as Thomas ˆ Kempis. The treatise should be read by all, as one of the very best devotional works in any language. My only reason for not translating it in full here is that a good English translation already exists,[30] so that it seemed unnecessary to offer a new one to the public. I have therefore only translated a few characteristic passages, which are very far from exhausting its beauties, and a few of the more striking aphorisms, which indicate the main points in the religious philosophy of the writer.

Sect. 9. MODERN MYSTICISM

The revival of interest in the old mystical writers is not surprising when we consider the whole trend of modern thought. Among recent philosophers-- though Lotze, perhaps the greatest name among them, is unsympathetic, in consequence of his over-rigid theory of personality--the great psychologist Fechner, whose religious philosophy is not so well known in this country as it deserves to be, has with some justice been called a mystic. And our own greatest living metaphysician, Mr F.H. Bradley, has expounded the dialectic of speculative mysticism with unequalled power, though with a bias against Christianity. Another significant fact is the great popularity, all over Europe, of Maeterlinck's mystical works, "Le Tr 閦 or des Humbles," "La Sagesse et la Destin 閑," and "Le Temple Enseveli."

The growing science of psychology has begun to turn its attention seriously to the study of the religious faculty. Several able men have set themselves to collect material which may form the basis of an inductive science. Personal experiences, communicated by many persons of both sexes and of various ages, occupations, and levels of culture, have been brought together and tabulated. It is claimed that important facts have already been established, particularly in connexion with the phenomena of conversion, by this method. The results have certainly been more than enough to justify confidence in the soundness of the method, and hope that the new science may have a great future before it. Towards mysticism, recent writers on the psychology of religion have been less favourable than the pure metaphysicians. While the latter have shown a tendency towards Pantheism and Determinism, which makes them sympathise with the general trend of speculative mysticism, psychology seems just at present to lean towards a pluralistic metaphysic and a belief in free-will or even in chance. This attitude is especially noticeable in the now famous Gifford Lectures of Professor William James[31] and in the recent volume of essays written at Oxford.[32] But even if the rising tide of neo-Kantianism should cause the speculative mystics to be regarded with disfavour, nothing can prevent the religion of the twentieth century from being mystical in type. The strongest wish of a vast number of earnest men and women to-day is for a basis of religious belief which shall rest, not upon tradition or external authority or historical evidence, but upon the ascertainable facts of human experience. The craving for immediacy, which we have seen to be characteristic of all mysticism, now takes the form of a desire to establish the validity of the God-consciousness as a normal part of the healthy inner life. We may perhaps venture to predict that the Christian biologist of the future will turn the Pauline Christology into his own dialect somewhat after the following fashion:--"The function of religion in the human race is closely analogous to, if not identical with, that of instinct in the lower animals. Religion is the racial will to live; not, however, to live anyhow and at all costs, but to live as human beings, conforming as far as possible to the highest type of humanity. Religion, therefore, acts as a higher instinct, inhibiting all self-destroying and race-destroying impulses in the interest of a larger self than the individual life." To turn this statement into theological form it is only necessary to claim that the "perfect man" which the religious instinct is trying to form is "the measure of the stature of the fulness of Christ," that that perfect humanity was once realised in the historical Christ, and that the higher instinct within us--ourselves, yet not ourselves--which makes for life and righteousness, and is the source of all the good that we can think, say, or do, may (in virtue of that historical incarnation) be justly called the indwelling Christ. This is all that the Christian mystic needs.

Sect. 10. SPECIMENS OF MODERN MYSTICISM

I conclude this introductory essay with a few extracts from recent American books on the psychology of religion. It is interesting to find some of the strangest experiences of the cloister reproduced under the very different conditions of modern American life. The quotations will serve to show how far Tauler and the "Theologia Germanica" are from being out of date.

"The thing which impressed me most" (says a correspondent of Professor William James)[33] "was learning the fact that we must be in absolutely constant relation or mental touch with that essence of life which permeates all and which we call God. This is almost unrecognisable unless we live into it ourselves actually--that is, by a constant turning to the very innermost, deepest consciousness of our real selves or of God in us, for illumination from within, just as we turn to the sun for light, warmth, and invigoration without. When you do this consciously, realising that to turn inward to the light within you is to live in the presence of God or of your Divine self, you soon discover the unreality of the objects to which you have hitherto been turning and which have engrossed you without."

The next quotation comes from a small book by one of the "New Thought" or "Mind Cure" school in America. The enormous sale of the volume testifies to the popularity of the teaching which it contains.[34]

"Intuition is an inner spiritual sense through which man is opened to the direct revelation and knowledge of God, the secret of nature and life, and through which he is brought into conscious unity and fellowship with God, and made to realise his own deific nature and supremacy of being as the son of God. Spiritual supremacy and illumination thus realised through the development and perfection of intuition under divine inspiration gives the perfect inner vision and direct insight into the character, properties, and purpose of all things to which the attention and interest are directed. It is, we repeat, a spiritual sense opening inwardly, as the physical senses open outwardly; and because it has the capacity to perceive, grasp, and know the truth at first hand, independent of all external sources of information, we call it intuition. All inspired teaching and spiritual revelations are based upon the recognition of this spiritual faculty of the soul and its power to receive and appropriate them. Conscious unity of man in spirit and purpose with the Father, born out of his supreme desire and trust, opens his soul through this inner sense to immediate aspiration and enlightenment from the divine omniscience, and the co-operative energy of the divine omnipotence, under which he becomes a seer and a master. On this higher plane of realised spiritual life in the flesh the mind acts with unfettered freedom and unbiassed vision, grasping truth at first hand, independent of all external sources of information. Approaching all beings and things from the divine side, they are seen in the light of the divine omniscience.[35] God's purpose in them, and so the truth concerning them, as it rests in the mind of God, are thus revealed by direct illumination from the divine mind, to which the soul is opened inwardly through this spiritual sense we call intuition."

The practice of meditation "without images," as the mediaeval mystics called it, is specially recommended. "Many will receive great help, and many will be entirely healed by a practice somewhat after the following nature:--With a mind at peace, and with a heart going out in love to all, go into the quiet of your own interior self, holding the thought, I am one with the Infinite Spirit of

Life, the life of my life. I now open my body, in which disease has gotten a foothold, I open it fully to the inflowing tide of this infinite life, and it now, even now, is pouring in and coursing through my body, and the healing process is going on." "If you would find the highest, the fullest, and the richest life that not only this world but that any world can know, then do away with the sense of the separateness of your life from the life of God. Hold to the thought of your oneness. In the degree that you do this, you will find yourself realising it more and more, and as this life of realisation is lived, you will find that no good thing will be withheld, for all things are included in this."[36]

This modern mysticism is very much entangled with theories about the cure of bodily disease by suggestion; and it is fair to warn those who are unacquainted with the books of this sect that they will find much fantastic superstition mixed with a stimulating faith in the inner light as the voice of God.

But whatever may be the course of this particular movement there can be no doubt that the Americans, like ourselves, are only at the beginning of a great revival of mystical religion. The movement will probably follow the same course as the mediaeval movement in Germany, with which this little book is concerned. It will have its philosophical supportees, who will press their speculation to the verge of Pantheism, perhaps reviving the Logos-cosmology of the Christian Alexandrians under the form of the pan-psychism of Lotze and Fechner. It will have its evangelists like Tauler, who will carry to our crowded town populations the glad tidings that the kingdom of God is not here or there, but within the hearts of all who will seek for it within them. It will assuredly attract some to a life of solitary contemplation; while others, intellectually weaker or less serious, will follow the various theosophical and theurgical delusions which, from the days of Iamblichus downward, have dogged the heels of mysticism. For the "False Light" against which the "Theologia Germanica" warns us is as dangerous as ever; we may even live to see some new "Brethren of the Free Spirit" turning their liberty into a cloak of licentiousness. If so, the world will soon whistle back the disciplinarian with his traditions of the elders; prophesying will once more be suppressed and discredited, and a new crystallising process will begin. But before that time comes some changes may possibly take place in the external proportions of Christian orthodoxy. The appearance of a vigorous body of faith, standing firmly on its own feet, may even have the effect of relegating to the sphere of pious opinion some tenets which have hitherto "seemed to be pillars."

For these periodical returns to the "fresh springs" of religion never leave the tradition exactly where it was before. The German movement of the fourteenth century made the Reformation inevitable, and our own age may be inaugurating a change no less momentous, which will restore in the twentieth century some of the features of Apostolic Christianity.

LIGHT, LIFE AND LOVE

ECKHART

GOD

GOD is nameless, for no man can either say or understand aught about Him. If I say, God is good, it is not true; nay more; I am good, God is not good. I may even say, I am better than God; for whatever is good, may become better, and whatever may become better, may become best. Now God is not good, for He cannot become better. And if He cannot become better, He cannot become best, for these three things, good, better, and best, are far from God, since He is above all. If I also say, God is wise, it is not true; I am wiser than He. If I also say, God is a Being, it is not true; He is transcendent Being and superessential Nothingness. Concerning this St Augustine says: the best thing that man can say about God is to be able to be silent about Him, from the wisdom of his inner judgement. Therefore be silent and prate not about God, for whenever thou dost prate about God, thou liest, and committest sin. If thou wilt be without sin, prate not about God. Thou canst understand nought about God, for He is above all understanding. A master saith: If I had a God whom I could understand, I would never hold Him to be God. (318)[37]

God is not only a Father of all good things, as being their First Cause and Creator, but He is also their Mother, since He remains with the creatures which have from Him their being and existence, and maintains them continually in their being. If God did not abide with and in the creatures, they must necessarily have fallen back, so soon as they were created, into the nothingness out of which they were created. (610)

REST ONLY IN GOD

IF I had everything that I could desire, and my finger ached, I should not have everything, for I should have a pain in my finger, and so long as that remained, I should not enjoy full comfort. Bread is comfortable for men, when they are hungry; but when they are thirsty, they find no more comfort in bread than in a stone. So it is with clothes, they are welcome to men, when they are cold; but when they are too hot, clothes give them no comfort. And so it is with all the creatures. The comfort which they promise is only on the surface, like froth, and it always carries with it a want. But God's comfort is clear and has nothing wanting: it is full and complete, and God is constrained to give it thee, for He cannot cease till He have given thee Himself. (300)

It is only in God that are collected and united all the perfections, which in the creatures are sundered and divided. (324)

Yet all the fulness of the creatures can as little express God, as a drop of water can express the sea. (173)

GOD IS ALWAYS READY

NO one ought to think that it is difficult to come to Him, though it sounds difficult and is really difficult at the beginning, and in separating oneself from and dying to all things. But when a man has once entered upon it, no life is lighter or happier or more desirable; for God is very zealous to be at all times with man, and teaches him that He will bring him to Himself if man will but follow. Man never desires anything so earnestly as God desires to bring a man to Himself, that he may know Him. God is always ready, but we are very unready; God is near to us, but we are far from Him; God is within, but we are without; God is at home, but we are strangers. The prophet saith: God guideth the redeemed through a narrow way into the broad road, so that they come into the wide and broad place; that is to say, into true freedom of the spirit, when one has become a spirit with God. May God help us to follow this course, that He may bring us to Himself. Amen. (223)

GRACE

THE masters say: That is young, which is near its beginning. Intelligence is the youngest faculty in man: the first thing to break out from the soul is intelligence, the next is will, the other faculties follow. Now he saith: Young man, I say unto thee, arise. The soul in itself is a simple work; what God works in the simple light of the soul is more beautiful and more delightful than all the other works which He works in all creatures. But foolish people take evil for good and good for evil. But to him who rightly understands, the one work which God works in the soul is better and nobler and higher than all the world. Through that light comes grace. Grace never comes in the intelligence or in the will. If it could come in the intelligence or in the will, the intelligence and the will would have to transcend themselves. On this a master says: There is something secret about it; and thereby he means the spark of the soul, which alone can apprehend God. The true union between God and the soul takes place in the little spark, which is called the spirit of the soul. Grace unites not to any work. It is an indwelling and a living together of the soul in God. (255)

Every gift of God makes the soul ready to receive a new gift, greater than itself. (15)

Yea, since God has never given any gift, in order that man might rest in the possession of the gift, but gives every gift that He has given in heaven and on earth, in order that He might be able to give one gift, which is Himself, so with this gift of grace, and with all His gifts He will make us ready for the one gift, which is Himself. (569)

No man is so boorish or stupid or awkward, that he cannot, by God's grace, unite his will wholly and entirely with God's will. And nothing more is necessary than that he should say with earnest longing: O Lord, show me Thy dearest will, and strengthen me to do it. And God does it, as sure as He lives, and gives him grace in ever richer fulness, till he comes to perfection, as He gave to the woman at Jacob's well. Look you, the most ignorant and the lowest of you all can obtain this from God, before he leaves this church, yea, before I finish this sermon, as sure as God lives and I am a man. (187)

O almighty and merciful Creator and good Lord, be merciful to me for my poor sins, and help me that I may overcome all temptations and shameful lusts, and may be able to avoid utterly, in thought and deed, what Thou forbiddest, and give me grace to do and to hold all that Thou hast commanded. Help me to believe, to hope, and to love, and in every way to live as Thou willest, as much as Thou willest, and what Thou willest. (415)

THE WILL

THEN is the will perfect, when it has gone out of itself, and is formed in the will of God. The more this is so, the more perfect and true is the will, and in such a will thou canst do all things. (553)

SURRENDER OF THE WILL

YOU should know, that that which God gives to those men who seek to do His will with all their might, is the best. Of this thou mayest be as sure, as thou art sure that God lives, that the very best must necessarily be, and that in no other way could anything better happen. Even if something else seems better, it would not be so good for thee, for God wills this and not another way, and this way must be the best for thee. Whether it be sickness or poverty or hunger or thirst, or whatever it be, that God hangs over thee or does not hang over thee--whatever God gives or gives not, that is all what is best for thee; whether it be devotion or inwardness, or the lack of these which grieves thee--only set thyself right in this, that thou desirest the glory of God in all things, and then whatever He does to thee, that is the best.

Now thou mayest perchance say: How can I tell whether it is the will of God or not? If it were not the will of God, it would not happen. Thou couldst have neither sickness nor anything else unless God willed it. But know that it is God's will that thou shouldst have so much pleasure and satisfaction therein, that thou shouldst feel no pain as pain; thou shouldst take it from God as the very best thing, for it must of necessity be the very best thing for thee. Therefore I may even wish for it and desire it, and nothing would become me better than so to do.

If there were a man whom I were particularly anxious to please, and if I knew for certain that he liked me better in a grey cloak than in any other, there is no doubt that however good another cloak might be, I should be fonder of the grey than of all the rest. And if there were anyone whom I would gladly please,

I should do nothing else in word or deed than what I knew that he liked.

Ah, now consider how your love shows itself! If you loved God, of a surety nothing would give you greater pleasure than what pleases Him best, and that whereby His will may be most fully done. And, however great thy pain or hardship may be, if thou hast not as great pleasure in it as in comfort or fulness, it is wrong.

We say every day in prayer to our Father, Thy will be done. And yet when His will is done, we grumble at it, and find no pleasure in His will. If our prayers were sincere, we should certainly think His will, and what He does, to be the best, and that the very best had happened to us. (134)

Those who accept all that the Lord send, as the very best, remain always in perfect peace, for in them God's will has become their will. This is incomparably better than for our will to become God's will. For when thy will becomes God's will--if thou art sick, thou wishest not to be well contrary to God's will, but thou wishest that it were God's will that thou shouldest be well. And so in other things. But when God's will becomes thy will--then thou art sick: in God's name; thy friend dies: in God's name! (55)

SUFFERING

MEN who love God are so far from complaining of their sufferings, that their complaint and their suffering is rather because the suffering which God's will has assigned them is so small. All their blessedness is to suffer by God's will, and not to have suffered something, for this is the loss of suffering. This is why I said, Blessed are they who are willing to suffer for righteousness, not, Blessed are they who have suffered. (434)

All that a man bears for God's sake, God makes light and sweet for him. (45)

If all was right with you, your sufferings would no longer be suffering, but love and comfort. (442)

If God could have given to men anything more noble than suffering, He would have redeemed mankind with it: otherwise, you must say that my Father was my enemy, if he knew of anything nobler than suffering. (338)

True suffering is a mother of all the virtues. (338)

SIN

DEADLY sin is a death of the soul. To die is to lose life. But God is the life of the soul; since then deadly sin separates us from God, it is a death of the soul.

Deadly sin is also an unrest of the heart. Everything can rest only in its proper place. But the natural place of the soul is God; as St Augustine says, Lord, thou hast made us for Thyself, and our heart is restless till it finds rest in Thee. But deadly sin separates us from God; therefore it is an unrest of the heart. Deadly sin is also a sickness of the faculties, when a man can never stand up alone for the weight of his sins, nor ever resist falling into sin. Therefore deadly sin is a sickness of the faculties. Deadly sin is also a blindness of the sense, in that it suffers not a man to know the shortness of the pleasures of lust, nor the length of the punishment in hell, nor the eternity of joys in heaven. Deadly sin is also a death of all graces; for as soon as a deadly sin takes place, a man becomes bare of all graces. (217)

Every creature must of necessity abide in God; if we fall out of the hands of his mercy, we fall into the hands of His justice. We must ever abide in Him. What madness then is it to wish not to be with Him, without whom thou canst not be! (169)

CONTENTMENT

A GREAT teacher once told a story in his preaching about a man who for eight years besought God to show him a man who would make known to him the way of truth. While he was in this state of anxiety there came a voice from God and spake to him: Go in front of the church, and there shalt thou find a man who will make known to thee the way of truth. He went, and found a poor man whose feet were chapped and full of dirt, and all his clothes were hardly worth twopence-halfpenny. He greeted this poor man and said to him, God give thee a good morning. The poor man answered, I never had a bad morning. The other said, God give thee happiness. How answerest thou that? The poor man answered, I was never unhappy. The first then said, God send thee blessedness. How answerest thou that? I was never unblessed, was the answer. Lastly the questioner said, God give thee health! Now enlighten me, for I cannot understand it. And the poor man replied, When thou saidst to me, may God give thee a good morning, I said I never had a bad morning. If I am hungry, I praise God for it; if I am cold, I praise God for it; if I am distressful and despised, I praise God for it; and that is why I never had a bad morning. When thou askedst God to give me happiness, I answered that I had never been unhappy; for what God gives or ordains for me, whether it be His love or suffering, sour or sweet, I take it all from God as being the best, and that is why I was never unhappy. Thou saidst further, May God make thee blessed, and I said, I was never unblessed, for I have given up my will so entirely to God's will, that what God wills, that I also will, and that is why I was never unblessed, because I willed alone God's will. Ah! dear fellow, replied the man; but if God should will to throw thee into hell, what wouldst thou say then? He replied, Throw me into hell! Then I would resist Him. But even if He threw me into hell, I should still have two arms wherewith to embrace Him. One arm is true humility, which I should place under Him, and with the arm of love I should embrace Him. And he concluded, I would rather be in hell and possess God, than in the kingdom of heaven without Him. (623)

DETACHMENT

THE man who has submitted his will and purposes entirely to God, carries God with him in all his works and in all circumstances. Therein can no man hinder him, for he neither aims at nor enjoys anything else, save God. God is united with Him in all his purposes and designs. Even as no manifoldness can dissipate God, so nothing can dissipate such a man, or destroy his unity. Man, therefore, should take God with him in all things; God should be always present to his mind and will and affections. The same disposition that thou hast in church or in thy cell, thou shouldst keep and maintain in a crowd, and amid the unrest and manifoldness of the world.

Some people pride themselves on their detachment from mankind, and are glad to be alone or in church; and therein lies their peace. But he who is truly in the right state, is so in all circumstances, and among all persons; he who is not in a good state, it is not right with him in all places and among all persons. He who is as he should be has God with him in truth, in all places and among all persons, in the street as well as in the church; and then no man can hinder him. (547)

It is often much harder for a man to be alone in a crowd than in the desert; and it is often harder to leave a small thing than a great, and to practise a small work than one which people consider very great. (565)

PRAYER

GOOD and earnest prayer is a golden ladder which reaches up to heaven, and by which man ascends to God.

The man who will pray aright should ask for nothing except what may promote God's honour and glory, his own profit and the advantage of his neighbours. When we ask for temporal things we should always add, if it be God's will and if it be for my soul's health. But when we pray for virtues, we need add no qualification, for these are God's own working. (359)

LOVE OF OUR NEIGHBOUR

IT is a hard thing to practise this universal love, and to love our neighbours as ourselves, as our Lord commanded us. But if you will understand it rightly, there is a greater reward attached to this command, than to any other. The commandment seems hard, but the reward is precious indeed. (135)

LOVE

HE who has found this way of love, seeketh no other. He who turns on this pivot is in such wise a prisoner that his foot and hand and mouth and eyes and heart, and all his human faculties, belong to God. And, therefore, thou canst overcome thy flesh in no better way, so that it may not shame thee, than by love. This is why it is written, Love is as strong as death, as hard as hell. Death separates the soul from the body, but love separates all things from the soul. She suffers nought to come near her, that is not God nor God-like. Happy is he who is thus imprisoned; the more thou art a prisoner, the more wilt thou be freed. That we may be so imprisoned, and so freed, may He help us, Who Himself is Love. (30)

THE UNION WITH GOD

THE union of the soul with God is far more inward than that of the soul and body. (566)

Now I might ask, how stands it with the soul that is lost in God? Does the soul find herself or not? To this will I answer as it appears to me, that the soul finds herself in the point, where every rational being understands itself with itself. Although it sinks and sinks in the eternity of the Divine Essence, yet it can never reach the ground. Therefore God has left a little point wherein the soul turns back upon itself and finds itself, and knows itself to be a creature. (387)

God alone must work in thee without hindrance, that He may bring to perfection His likeness in thee. So thou mayest understand with Him, and love with Him. This is the essence of perfection. (471)

THE LAST JUDGMENT

PEOPLE say of the last day, that God shall give judgment. This is true. But it is not true as people imagine. Every man pronounces his own sentence; as he shows himself here in his essence, so will he remain everlastingly. (471)

PRECEPT AND PRACTICE

BETTER one life-master than a thousand reading-masters (wger wre ein lebemeister denne t 鷄 ent lesemeister). If I sought a master in the scriptures, I should seek him in Paris and in the high schools of high learning. But if I wished to ask questions about the perfect life, that he could not tell me. Where then must I go? Nowhere at all save to an utterly simple nature; he could answer my question. (599)

RELICS

MY people, why seek ye after dead bones? Why seek ye not after living holiness, which might give you everlasting life? The dead can neither give nor take away. (599)

SAYINGS OF ECKHART

MASTER ECKHART saith: He who is always alone, he is worthy of God; and he who is always at home, to him is God present; and be who abides always in a present now, in him doth God beget His Son without ceasing. (600)

Master Eckhart saith: I will never pray to God to give Himself to me: I will pray Him to make me purer. If I were purer, God must give Himself to me, of His own nature, and sink into me. (601)

Master Eckhart was asked, what were the greatest goods, that God had done to him. He said, there are three. The first is, that the lusts and desires of the flesh have been taken away from me. The second is, that the Divine Light shines and gives me light in all my doings. The third is, that I am daily renewed in virtue, grace and holiness. (602)

TAULER

OUR AIM

THINK, and think earnestly, how great, how unutterable will be the joy and blessedness, the glory and honour of those who shall see clearly and without veil the gladsome and beauteous face of God, how they will enjoy the best and highest good, which is God Himself. For in Him is included all pleasure, might, joy, and all beauty, so that the blessed in God will possess everything that is good and desirable, with everlasting joy and security, without fear lest they should ever be parted from Him. (138)[38]

CONSEQUENCES OF THE FALL

FROM the time when the first man gave a ready ear to the words of the enemy, mankind have been deaf, so that none of us can hear or understand the loving utterances of the eternal Word. Something has happened to the ears of man, which has stopped up his ears, so that he cannot hear the loving Word; and he has also been so blinded, that he has become stupid, and does not know himself. If he wished to speak of his own inner life, he could not do it; he knows not where he is, nor what is his state. (91)

How can it be that the noble reason, the inner eye, is so blinded that it cannot see the true light? This great shame has come about, because a thick coarse skin and a thick fur has been drawn over him, even the love and the opinion of the creatures, whether it be the man himself or something that belongs to him; hence man has become blind and deaf, in whatever position he may be, worldly or spiritual. Yes, that is his guilt, that many a thick skin is drawn over him, as thick as an ox's forehead, and it has so covered up his inner man, that neither God nor himself can get inside; it has grown into him. (92)

THE FALL

THROUGH two things man fell in Paradise--through pride, and through inordinate affection. Therefore we too must return by two things, that nature may recover her power: we must first sink our nature and bring it down under God and under all men in deep humility, against whom it had exalted itself in pride. We must also manfully die to all inordinate lusts. (1)

LIFE A BATTLE

NOTHING in the world is so necessary for man as to be constantly assailed; for in fighting he learns to know himself. As grace is necessary to a man, so also is fighting. Virtue begins in fighting, and is developed in fighting. In every state to which a man is called, inward and outward, he must of necessity be assailed. A high Master said: As little as meat can remain without salt and yet not become corrupt, so little can a man remain without fighting. (104)

A man should in the first place act as when a town is besieged, and it is certain that the besieging army is stronger than the town. When the town is weakest, men take the very greatest care to guard and defend the town; if they neglected to do so, they would lose the town, and with it their lives and properties. So should every man do: he should be most careful to find out in what things the evil spirit most often besets him--that is, on what side the man is weakest, and to what kind of errors and failings he is most prone, and should manfully defend himself at those points.

Next, turn thyself earnestly away from sin; for I tell you of a truth, by whatever temptation a man is assailed, if he turns not from it heartily, but stands in it vacillating, he has no wholehearted desire to leave his sins by God's will, and without doubt the evil spirit is close upon him, who may make him fall into endless perdition.

Know of a truth, that if thou wouldst truly overcome the evil spirit, this can only be done by a complete manful turning away from sin. Say then with all thy heart: Oh, everlasting God, help me and give me Thy Divine grace to be my help, for it is my steadfast desire never again to commit any deadly sin against Thy Divine will and Thine honour. So with thy good will and intention thou entirely overcomest the evil spirit, so that he must fly from thee ashamed.

Understand, however, that it is a miserable and pitiable thing for a reasonable man to let himself be overcome by the evil spirit, and in consequence of his attacks to fall voluntarily into grievous and deadly sin, whereby man loses the grace of God. A reasonable man, who allows himself voluntarily to be overcome by the evil spirit, is like a well-armed man who voluntarily lets a fly bite him to death. For man has many great and strong weapons, wherewith he may well and manfully withstand the evil spirit--the holy faith, the blessed sacrament, the holy word of God, the model and example of all good and holy men, the prayers of holy Church, and other great supports against the power of the evil spirit, whose power is much less than that of a fly against a great bear. If a man will manfully and boldly withstand the evil spirit, the evil one can gain no advantage against his free will.

Turn, therefore, manfully and earnestly from your sins, and watch diligently and earnestly; for I tell you of a truth, that when you have come to the next world, if you have not withstood the evil spirit, and if you are found there without repentance and sorrow, you will be a mockery to all the devils and to yourself, and you will be eternally punished and tormented. And it will then be a greater woe to you, that you have followed the evil spirit, than all the external pains that you must endure eternally for your sins.

Thirdly, a man should diligently attend to his inner Ground, that there shall be nothing in it save God alone, and His eternal glory. For alas! there are many men, both lay and clerical, who live falsely beneath a fair show, and imagine that they can deceive the everlasting God. No, in truth, thou deceivest thyself, and losest the day of grace, and the favour of God, and makest thyself guilty towards God, in that He gives the evil spirits power over thee, so that thou canst do no good work. Therefore, watch while it is day, that the hour of darkness and God's disfavour may not overtake thee, and take heed that in thy inner ground God may dwell, and nought besides. (75)

Even as each man in his baptism is placed under the charge of a special angel, who is with him always and never leaves him, and protects him waking and sleeping in all his ways and in all his works, so every man has a special devil, who continually opposes him and exercises him without ceasing. But if the man were wise and diligent, the opposition of the devil and his exercises would be much more profitable to him than the aid of the good angel; for if there were no struggle, there could be no victory. (139)

SIN

WHEN a man has had the fair net of his soul torn by sin, he must patch and mend it by a humble, repentant return to the grace and mercy of God. He must act like one who wishes to make a crooked stick straight: he bends the stick further back than it ought to go, and by being thus bent back it becomes straight again. So must a man do to his own nature. He must bend himself under all things which belong to God, and break himself right off, inwardly and outwardly, from all things which are not God.

Every deadly sin causes the precious blood of Christ to be shed afresh. Jesus Christ is spiritually crucified many times every day. (75)

FISHING FOR SOULS

THE fisherman throws his hook, that he may catch the fish; but the fish itself takes the hook. When the fish takes the hook, the fisherman is sure of the fish, and draws it to him. Even so, God has thrown His hook and His net into all the world, before our feet, before our eyes, before our minds, and He would gladly draw us securely to Himself by means of all His creatures. By pleasurable things He draws us on; by painful things He drives us on. He who will not be drawn, is in fault; for he has not taken God's hook, nor will he be caught in God's net. If he came therein, beyond doubt he would be caught by God and would be drawn by God. It is not God's fault if we will not be drawn; we should grasp the hand held out to us. If a man were in a deep pool, and one tried to help him and pull him out, would he not gladly grasp his hand and allow himself to be pulled out? (42)

Where two things are so related to each other, that one may receive something for the other, there must be something in common between them. If they had nothing in common, there must be a middle term between them, which has something in common both with the higher, from which it may receive, and with the lower, to which it may impart. Now God hath created all things, and especially mankind, immediately for Himself. He created man for His pleasure. But by sin, human nature was so far estranged from God, that it was impossible for a man to attain to that, for which he was made. Now Aristotle says that God and Nature are not unprofitable workers--that is, what they work at, they carry to its end. Now God created man that He might have pleasure in him. If then God's work in creating mankind was not to be unprofitable, when they were so far estranged from God by sin, that they could not receive that by which they might return and attain the enjoyment of eternal happiness, a Mediator was necessary between us and God, one who has something in common with us and our natures, and also shares in the nature of God. In order that on the one side, He might in Himself destroy our sickness, which was a cause of all our sins, and also destroy all our sins, to which our weakness has brought us; and on the other side that He might include in Himself all the treasure of grace and of God's honour, that He might be able to give us grace richly, and forgiveness of our sins, and eternal glory hereafter, this could only be, if the Son of God became man. (90)

Yea, the highest God and Lord of all lords, the Son of God, in His deep love felt pity for us poor, sinful men, condemned to the flames of hell. Though He was in the form of God, He thought it not robbery (as St Paul says) to be equal with God, and He annihilated Himself, and took upon Him the form of a servant, and was made like any other man, being found in fashion as a man. He humbled Himself, and became obedient unto death, even the death of the cross. (117)

THE EFFICACY OF DIVINE GRACE

ALL works which men and all creatures can ever work even to the end of the world, without the grace of God--all of them together, however great they may be, are an absolute nothing, as compared with the smallest work which God has worked in men by His grace. As much as God is better than all His creatures, so much better are His works than all the works, or wisdom, or designs, which all men could devise. Even the smallest drop of grace is better than all earthly riches that are beneath the sun. Yea, a drop of grace is more noble than all angels and all souls, and all the natural things that God has made. And yet grace is given more richly by God to the soul than any earthly gift. It is given more richly than brooks of water, than the breath of the air, than the brightness of the sun; for spiritual things are far finer and nobler than earthly things. The whole Trinity, Father, Son, and Holy Ghost, give grace to the soul, and flow immediately into it; even the highest angel, in spite of his great nobility, cannot do this. Grace looses us from the snares of many temptations; it relieves us from the heavy burden of worldly cares, and carries the spirit up to heaven, the land of spirits. It kills the worm of conscience, which makes sins alive. Grace is a very powerful thing. The man, to whom cometh but a little drop of the light of grace, to him all that is not God becomes as bitter as gall upon the tongue. (86)

Grace makes, contrary to nature, all sorrows sweet, and brings it about that a man no longer feels any relish for things which formerly gave him great pleasure and delight. On the other hand, what formerly disgusted him, now delights him and is the desire of his heart--for instance, weakness, sorrow, inwardness, humility, self-abandonment, and detachment from all the creatures. All this is in the highest degree dear to him, when this visitation of the Holy Ghost, grace, has in truth come to him. Then the sick man, that is to say the external man, with all his faculties is plunged completely into the pool of water, even as the sick man who had been for thirty-eight years by the pool at Jerusalem, and there washes himself thoroughly in the exalted, noble, precious blood of Christ Jesus. For grace in manifold ways bathes the soul in the wounds and blood of the holy Lamb, Jesus Christ. (22)

PRAYER

THE essence of prayer is the ascent of the mind to God, as holy teachers tell us. Therefore every good man, when he wishes to pray, ought to collect his outer senses into himself, and look into his mind, to see whether it be really turned to God. He who wishes that his prayers may be truly heard, must keep himself turned away from all temporal and external things, and all that is not

Divine, whether it be friend or joy (Freund oder Freude), and all vanities, whether they be clothes or ornaments, and from everything of which God is not the true beginning and ending, and from everything that does not belong to Him. He must cut off his words and his conduct, his manners and his demeanour, from all irregularity, inward or outward. Dream not that that can be a true prayer, when a man only babbles outwardly with his mouth, and reads many psalms, gabbling them rapidly and hastily, while his mind wanders this way and that, backwards and forwards. Much rather must the true prayer be, as St Peter tells us, "one-minded"[39]—that is, the mind must cleave to God alone, and a man must look with the face of his soul turned directly towards God, with a gentle, willing dependence on Him. (80)

If thy prayer has these conditions, thou mayst with true humility fall at the feet of God, and pray for the gentle succour of God; thou mayest knock at His fatherly heart, and ask for bread—that is, for love. If a man had all the food in the world, and had not bread, his food would be neither eatable, nor pleasant, nor useful. So it is with all things, without the Love of God. Knock also at the door through which we must go--namely, Christ Jesus. At this door, the praying man must knock for three ends, if he wishes to be really admitted. First he must knock devoutly, at the broken heart and the open side, and enter in with all devotion, and in recognition of his unfathomable poverty and nothingness, as poor Lazarus did at the rich man's gate, and ask for crumbs of His grace. Then again, he should knock at the door of the holy open wounds of His holy hands, and pray for true Divine knowledge, that it may enlighten him and exalt him. Finally, knock at the door of His holy feet, and pray for true Divine love, which may unite thee with Him, and immerse and cover thee in Him. (57)

MEDITATIONS ON THE SEVEN WORDS FROM THE CROSS

[From a devotional treatise on the Passion of Christ, published in a Latin translation, by Surius, in 1548, and wrongly ascribed by him to Tauler. The author was an unknown German of the fourteenth century.]

THE FIRST WORD

NOW, O my soul, and all ye who have been redeemed by the precious blood of Christ, come, and let us go with inward compassion and fervent devotion to the blessed palm-tree of the Cross, which is laden with the fairest fruit. Let us pass like the bee from flower to flower, for all are full of honey. Let us consider and ponder with the greatest care the sacred words of Christ, which He spoke upon the Cross; for everything that comes From this blessed Tree is wholesome and good. In the Cross of our Lord and Saviour are centred all our salvation, all our health, all our life, all our glory; and, "if we suffer with Him," saith the Apostle, "we shall also reign with Him." That we may not be found ungrateful for these inestimable benefits, let us call upon heaven and earth, and all that in them is, to join us in praising and blessing and giving thanks to God. Let us invite them to come and look upon this wondrous sight, and say: "Magnify the Lord with me, for He hath done marvellous things. O praise and bless the Lord with me, for great is His mercy toward us." Come up with me, I pray you, ye angelic spirits, to Mount Calvary, and see your King Solomon on His throne, wearing the diadem wherewith His mother has crowned Him. Let us weep in the presence of the Lord who made us, the Lord our God. O all mankind, and all ye who are members of Christ, behold your Redeemer as He hangs on high; behold and weep. See if any sorrow is like unto His sorrow. Acknowledge the heinousness of your sins, which needed such satisfaction. Go to every part of His body; you will find only wounds and blood. Cry to Him with lamentations and say, "O Jesus, our redemption, our love, our desire, what mercy has overcome Thee, that Thou shouldest bear our sins, and endure a cruel death, to rescue us from everlasting death?" And Thou, O God, the almighty Father of heaven, look down from Thy sanctuary upon Thine innocent Son Joseph, sold and given over unjustly to the hands of bloody men, to suffer a shameful death. See whether this be Thy Son's coat or not. Of a truth an evil beast hath devoured Him. The blood of our sins is sprinkled over His garments, and all the coverings of His good name are defiled by it. See how Thy holy Child has been condemned with the wicked, how Thy royal Son has been crowned with thorns. Behold His innocent hands, which have known no sin, dripping with blood; behold His sacred feet, which have never turned aside from the path of justice, pierced through by a cruel nail; behold His defenceless side smitten with a sharp spear; behold His fair face, which the angels desire to look upon, marred and shorn of all its beauty; behold His blessed heart, which no impure thought ever stained, weighed down with inward sorrow. Behold, O loving Father, Thy sweet Son, stretched out upon the harp of the Cross, and harping blessings on Thee with all His members. Wherefore, O my God, I pray Thee to forgive me, for the sake of Thy Son's Passion, all the sins that I have committed in my members. O merciful Father, look on Thy only-begotten Son, that Thou mayst have compassion on Thy servant. Whenever that red blood of Thy Son speaks in Thy sight, do Thou wash me from every stain of sin. Whenever Thou beholdest the wounds of this Thy Son, open to me the bosom of Thy fatherly compassion. Behold, O tender Father, how Thy obedient Son does not cry, "Bind my hands and my feet, that I may not rebel against Thee," but how of His own will He extends His hands and feet, and gladly allows them to be pierced with nails. Look down, I pray Thee, not on the brazen serpent hanging on a pole for the salvation of Israel, but on Thine only Son hanging on the Cross for the salvation of all men. It is not Moses who now stretches out his hand to heaven, that the thunder and lightning and the other plagues may cease, but it is Thy beloved Son, who lovingly stretches out His bleeding arms to Thee, that Thy wrath may depart from the human race. Aaron and Hur are not now holding up the hands of Moses that he may pray more unweariedly for Israel; but hard and cruel nails have fastened the hands of Thy only Son to the Cross, that He may wait with long-suffering for our repentance, and receive us back into His grace, and that He may not turn away in wrath from our prayers. This is that faithful David, who now strings tight the harp-strings of His body, and makes sweet melody before Thee, singing to Thee the sweetest song that has been ever sung to Thee: "Father forgive them, for they know not what they do." This is that High Priest, who by His own blood has entered into the Holy of Holies, to offer Himself as a peace-offering for the sins of the whole world. This is that innocent Lamb, who has washed us in His own precious blood, who, Himself without spot of sin, has taken away the sins of the world. Therefore from the storehouse of His Passion I borrow the price of my debt, and I count out before Thee all its merits, to pay what I owe Thee. For He has done all in my nature, and for my sake. O merciful Father, if Thou weighest all my sins on one side of the balance, and in the other scale the Passion of Thy Son, the last will outweigh the first. For what sin can be so great, that the innocent blood of Thy Son has not washed it out? What pride, or disobedience, or lust, is so unchecked or so rebellious, that such lowliness, obedience, and poverty cannot abolish it? O merciful Father, accept the deeds of Thy beloved Son, and forgive the errors of Thy wicked servant. For the innocent blood of our brother Abel crieth to Thee from the Cross, not for vengeance, but for grace and mercy, saying, "Father, forgive them, for they know not what they do."

THE SECOND WORD

NOW the thieves who were crucified with Jesus reviled Him. But after a while, the one who hung on the right side of Christ, when he saw His great patience and long-suffering, wherewith He so lovingly prayed to His Father for those who cast reproaches upon Him and cruelly tortured Him, became entirely changed, and began to be moved with very great sorrow and repentance for his sins. And he showed this outwardly, when he rebuked his fellow-thief, who continued to revile Christ, saying: "Dost not thou fear God, seeing thou art in the same condemnation?" "Although" (he would say) "thou art so obstinate as not to fear men, and thinkest nought of thy bodily pain, yet surely thou must fear God, in the last moments of thy life--God, who hath power to destroy both thy body and soul in hell. And though we suffer the same punishment with Him, our deserts are very different. We, indeed, suffer justly, for we receive the due reward of our deeds, but this man hath done nothing amiss." He, who but lately was a blasphemer, is now a confessor and preacher, he distinguishes good from evil, blaming the sinner, and excusing the innocent: the unbelieving thief has become the confessor of almighty God. O good Jesus, this sudden change is wrought by Thy right hand, at which he hung. Thy right hand touched him inwardly, and forthwith he is changed into another man. O Lord, in this Thou hast declared Thy patience, out of a stone Thou hast raised up a child unto Abraham. Verily, the penitent thief received the light of faith solely from that bright light on the candlestick of the Cross, which shone there in the darkness and scattered the shades of night. But what does this signify, save that our Lord Jesus, out of the greatness of His goodness, looked upon him with the eyes of His mercy, although He found no merit in him, except what it pleased Him out of His goodness to bestow? For as God gives to His elect, out of His goodness alone, what no one has a right to demand, so out of His justice He gives to the wicked what they deserve. For this cause David says: "He saved me because He desired me." And this is why the thief, before the Lord touched his heart with the beams of His grace and love, joined the other thief in reviling Christ, thus showing first what his own character was, and afterwards what was wrought in him by grace. At first he acted like the other, being, like him, a child of wrath; but when the precious blood of Christ was shed as the price of our redemption and paid to the Father for our debt, then the thief asked God to give him an alms for his good, and at once received it. For how can one alms diminish that inexhaustible treasure? How could our tender Lord, whose property is always to have mercy, have refused his request? Indeed He gave him more than he asked. Yet how could the thief escape the glow of the fire which was burning so near him? Truly this was the fire, which the Father had sent down from heaven to earth, which had long smouldered, but now, kindled anew, and fed by the wood of the Cross, and sprinkled with the oil of mercy, and fanned, as it were, by the reproaches and blasphemies of the Jews, sent up its flames to heaven, by which that thief was quite kindled and set on fire, and his love became as strong as death, so that he said: "I indeed suffer no grievous penalty, for it is less than I deserve; but that this innocent One, who has done no wrong, should be so tortured, contrary to justice and righteousness, this, truly, adds grievous sorrow to my sorrow." O splendid faith of this thief! He contemned all the punishment that might be inflicted on him: he feared not the rage of the people, who were barking like mad dogs against Jesus: he cared not for the chief priests: he feared not the executioners with their weapons and instruments of torture; but in the presence of them all, with a fearless heart he confessed that Christ was the true Son of God, and Lord of the whole world: and at the same time he confounded the Jews by confessing that He had done nothing amiss, and therefore that they had crucified Him unjustly. O wondrous faith! O mighty constancy! O amazing love of this poor thief, love that cast out all fear! He was indeed well drunken with that new wine which in the wine-press of the Cross had been pressed out of that sweet cluster, Jesus Christ, and therefore he confessed Christ without shame before all the people. At the very beginning of the Passion, the apostles and disciples had forsaken Christ and fled; even St Peter, frightened by the voice of one maidservant, had denied Christ. But this poor thief did not forsake Him even in death, but confessed Him to be the Lord of heaven in the presence of all those armed men. Who can do justice to the merits of this man? Who taught him so quickly that faith of his, and his clear knowledge of all the virtues, save the very Wisdom of the Father, Jesus Christ, who hung near him on the Cross? Him whom the Jews could not or would not know, in spite of the promises made to the patriarchs, the fulfilment of prophecies, the teaching of the Scriptures, and the interpretation of allegories, this poor thief learned to know by repentance. He confessed Christ to be the Son of God, though he saw Him full of misery, want, and torment, and dying from natural weakness. He confessed Him at a time when the apostles, who had seen His mighty works, denied Him. The nails were holding his hands and feet fixed to the cross; he had nothing free about him, except his heart and his tongue; yet he gave to God all that he could give to Him, and, in the words of Scripture, "with his heart he believed unto righteousness, and with his tongue he made confession of Christ unto salvation." O infinite and unsearchable mercy of God! For what manner of man was he when he was sent to the cross, and what when he left it? (Not that it was his own cross, that wrought this change, but the power of Christ crucified.) He came to the cross stained with the blood of his fellow-man; he was taken down from it cleansed by the blood of Christ. He came to the cross still savage and full of rage, and while he was upon it he became so meek and pitiful that he lamented for the sufferings of another more than for his own. One member only was left to him, and at the eleventh hour he came to work in God's vineyard, and yet so eagerly did he labour that he was the first to finish his work and receive his reward. Indeed he behaved like a just man; for he first accused himself and confessed his sins, saying, "and we, indeed, justly, for we receive the due reward of our deeds." Secondly, he excused Christ, and confessed that He was the Just One when he said "but this Man hath done nothing amiss." Thirdly, he showed brotherly love, for he said, "dost not thou fear God?" Fourthly, with all his members, or at least with all that he could offer, and with loving eyes and a devout heart and a humble spirit, he turned himself to Christ and prayed earnestly, "Lord, remember me when Thou comest into Thy Kingdom." How great was the justice and humility and resignation which he showed in this prayer, for he asked only for a little remembrance of himself, acknowledging that he was not worthy to ask for anything great. Nor did he pray for the safety of his body, for he gladly desired to die for his sins. It was more pleasant for him to die with Christ than to live any longer. Nor did he pray that our Lord would deliver him from the pains of hell, or of purgatory, nor did he ask for the kingdom of heaven; but he resigned himself entirely to the will of God, and offered himself altogether to Christ, to do what He would with him. In his humility he prayed for nothing except for grace and mercy, for which David also prayed when he said, "Deal with Thy servant according to Thy mercy." And therefore, because he had prayed humbly and wisely, the Eternal Wisdom, Who reads the hearts of all who pray, heard his prayer, and, opening wide the rich storehouse of His grace, bestowed upon him much more than he had dared to ask. O marvellous goodness of God! How plainly dost Thou declare in this, that Thou desirest not the death of a sinner, but rather that he should be converted and live. Now Thou hast manifested and fulfilled what Thou didst promise aforetime by Thy prophet: "When the wicked man shall mourn for his sins, I will remember his iniquity no more." Thou didst not impose upon him many years of severe penance, nor many sufferings in purgatory for the expiation of his sins; but just as if Thou hadst quite forgotten his crimes, and couldst see nothing in him but virtue, Thou didst say: "This day shalt thou be with Me in paradise." O immeasurable compassion of God! Our tender Lord forgot all the countless crimes which that poor thief had done, and forgave him when he repented, and gave so great and splendid a reward to the good which there was in him, small indeed though it was. Our loving God is very rich; He needs not our gifts; but He seeks for a heart which turns to Him with lowliness and resignation, such a heart as He found in this poor thief. For He says Himself: "turn to Me, and I will turn to you." And so when this thief so courageously and effectively turned to God, his prayer was at once not only accepted but answered. For our Lord did not reject his prayer, or say to him: "See how I hang here in torment, and I behold before My eyes My mother in sore affliction, and I have not yet spoken one word to her, so that to hear thee now would not be just." No, our Lord said nothing of this kind to the thief. Rather, He heard his prayer at once, and made answer in that sweet word, "Amen, I say unto thee, this day shalt thou be with Me in paradise." O tender goodness, O marvellous mercy of God! O great wisdom of the thief! He saw that the treasures of Christ were wide open, and were being scattered abroad. Who then should forbid him to take as much as would pay what he owed to his Lord? And O the accursed hardness of the impenitent thief, whom neither the rebuke of his associate, nor the patience of Christ, nor the many signs of love and mercy that shone forth in Christ, could melt or convert! He saw that alms were plentiful at the rich man's gate, that more was given than was asked for, and yet he was too proud and obstinate to ask. He saw that life and the kingdom of heaven were being granted, and yet he would not bend his heart to wish for them: therefore he shall not have them. He loved better revilings and curses, and they shall come unto him, and that for all eternity. These new first-fruits of the grape, which our Lord gathered on the wood of the Cross from our barren soil, by much sweat of His brow and much watering with His own precious blood, He sent with great joy as a precious gift to His heavenly Father, by His celestial messengers the holy angels. But if there is joy among the angels of God over one sinner that repenteth, how must they rejoice and exult at the salvation of this thief, of whom they had almost despaired? We can picture to ourselves with what joy the Father of heaven received these first-fruits of the harvest of His Son's Passion. But Christ Himself, though He felt some joy at the thief's conversion, was still more afflicted thereby, for by His wisdom He foresaw that this thief would be the cause of perdition to many, who would resolve to pass their whole lives in sin, hoping to obtain pardon and grace at the moment of death. Truly a most foolish hope, for nowhere in the Scriptures do we read that it has so happened to any man. In truth, they who seek after God only when they must, will not, it is to be feared, find Him near them in their time of need. In the meantime, none can trust too much in God, and no one has ever been forsaken by Him, who has turned to Him with his whole heart, and leant upon Him with loving confidence.

THE THIRD WORD

THERE stood also by the Cross of Jesus His most holy and ever-virgin mother Mary; not in order that His sufferings might thereby be lessened, but that they might be greatly augmented. For if any creature could have given consolation to the Lord while He hung on the Cross, no one could have done it so fitly as His blessed mother. But since it was God's will that Christ should die the most bitter of deaths, and end His Passion without any comfort or relief, but with true resignation, His mother's presence brought Him no consolation, but rather added to His sufferings, for her sufferings were thereby added to His, and this added yet more to His affliction. Who then, O good Jesus can discover by meditation how great was Thy inward grief, for Thou knowest the hearts of all, when Thou sawest all the body of Thy holy mother tortured by inward compassion, even as Thou wast tortured on the Cross, and her tender heart and maternal breast pierced with the sword of sharp sorrow, her face pale as death, telling the anguish of her soul, and almost dead, yet unable to die. When Thou beheldest her hot tears, flowing down abundantly like sweet rivers upon her gracious cheeks, and over all her face, all witnesses to Thee that she shared in Thy sorrow and love; when Thou heardest her sad laments, forced from her by the weight of her affliction; when Thou sawest that same tender mother, melted away with the heat of love, her strength quite failing her, worn out and exhausted by the pains of Thy Passion, which wasted her away; all this, truly, was a new affliction to Thee on the Cross; it was itself a new Cross. For Thou alone, by the spear of, Thy pity, didst explore the weight and grievousness of her woes, which to men are beyond comprehension. All this, indeed, greatly increased the pain of Thy Passion, because Thou wast crucified not only in Thy own body, but in Thy mother's heart; for her Cross was Thy Cross, and Thine was hers. O how bitter was Thy Passion, sweet Jesus! Great indeed was Thy outward suffering, but far more grievous was Thy inward suffering, which

Thy heart experienced at Thy mother's anguish. It was now, beyond doubt, that the sword of sorrow pierced her through, for the queen of martyrs was terribly and mortally wounded in that part which is impassible--that is, the soul; she bore the death of the Cross in that part which could not die, suffering all the more her grievous inward death, as outward death departed further from her. Who, O most loving mother, can recount or conceive in his mind the immeasurable sorrows of thy soul, or thine inward woes? Him whom thou didst bring forth without pain, as a blessed mother free from the curse of our first mother Eve, who instead of the pains of labour wast filled with joy of spirit, and who for thy refreshment didst listen to the sweet songs of the angels as they praised thy Son, thou hast now seen slain before thine eyes with the greatest cruelty and tyranny. How manifold was that sorrow of thine, which thou wast permitted to escape at His birth, when thou sawest thy blessed and only Son hanging in such torment on the Cross, in the presence of a cruel and furious crowd, who showered upon Him all the insults and contumely and shame that they could think of; when thou sawest Him whom thou didst bear in thy pure womb without feeling the burden, so barbarously stretched on the Cross, and pierced with nails; when thou sawest His sacred arms, with which He had so many times lovingly embraced thee, stretched out so that He could not move them, and covered with red blood, His adorable head pierced with sharp thorns, and His whole body one streaming wound, while thou wast not able to staunch or anoint any of those wounds. What must thy grief have been when thou sawest Him whom thou hadst so often laid on thy virgin bosom that He might rest, without anything on which to lean His sacred head; and Him whom thou hadst nourished with the milk of thy holy breasts, now vexed with vinegar and gall. O how thy maternal heart was oppressed when thou beheldest with thy pure eyes that fair face so piteously marred, so that there was no beauty in it, and nothing by which He could be distinguished. How did the wave of affliction beat against and overflow and overwhelm thy soul! Truly, if even a devout man cannot without unspeakable sorrow and pity revolve in his mind the Passion of thy Son, what must have been thy Cross, thy affliction, who wast His mother and sawest it all with thine eyes? If to many friends of God and to many who love Him, thy Son's Passion is as grievous as if they suffered it themselves, if by inward pity they are crucified with thy Son, how terribly, even unto death, must thou have been crucified inwardly, when thou didst not only ponder and search into the outward and inward pains of thy Son in thy devout heart, but sawest them with thy bodily eyes? For never did any mother love her child as thou lovedst thy Son. And if

St Paul, who loved so much, could say, out of his ardent love and deep pity for thy Son, "I am crucified with Christ; and I bear in my body the marks of the Lord Jesus," how much more wert thou crucified with Him, and didst inwardly receive all His wounds, being made, in a manner, an image and likeness of thy crucified Son?

THE FOURTH WORD

ABOUT the ninth hour our Lord Jesus cried with a loud voice, "My God, My God, why hast Thou forsaken Me?" He cried with a loud voice, that He might be easily heard by all, and also that by this wondrous word He might shake off from our souls the sleep of sloth, and cause them to wonder and marvel at the immeasurable goodness of God to us. Therefore He saith, "My God, My God, why hast Thou forsaken Me?" For the sake of vile sinners, for evil and thankless servants, for sinful and disobedient deceivers, Thou hast forsaken Thy beloved Son and most obedient Child. That Thy enemies, who are vessels of wrath, might be changed into children of adoption, Thou hast slain Thine own Son, and given Him over to death like one guilty. "O my God, why, I pray Thee, hast Thou forsaken me?" For the very cause why men ought to praise and give thanks to Thee, and love Thee with an everlasting love; because Thou hast delivered Thy dear Son to death for their redemption, and sacrificed Him willingly, for this reason they will find ground for blasphemy and reproach against Thee, saying, "He saith He is the Son of God. Let God deliver Him now if He will have Him." Why, O my God, hast Thou willed to spend so precious a treasure for such vile and counterfeit goods? Besides, this word may be understood to have been spoken by Christ against those who seek to diminish the glory of His Passion, by saying that it was not really so bitter and terrible, owing to the great support and comfort which He drew from His Godhead. Let those who speak and think thus know that they renew His Passion and crucify Him afresh. It was to prove the error of such men that our Lord cried with a loud voice, and said, "My God, My God, why hast Thou forsaken Me?" It is as if He had said these words to His own Divine nature, with which He formed one Person--for the Godhead of the Father and of the Son is all one--wondering, Himself, at His own love, which had so cast Him down and worn Him out and humbled Him, and that He who brings help to all mankind should have forsaken Himself, and offered Himself to suffer every kind of pain, impelled thereto by conquering love alone. Again, we should not be wrong, if we were to interpret this word which Christ spoke out of the exceeding bitterness of His sorrow in the following way--namely, that His spirit and inward man, taking upon itself the severe judgment of God upon all sinners, and at the same time discerning clearly and feeling and measuring in Himself the intolerable weight of His Passion, on this account cried out in a sorrowful voice to His Father, and complained tenderly to Him because He had been cast into these dreadful torments; as if the goodness of His Father had become so embittered against the sins of men, that in the ardour of His justice He had quite forgotten the inseparable union between His passible humanity and His impassible Godhead, and therefore in the zealousness of His justice had quite given up His passible nature to the cruelty and malice of fierce men, that they might waste it away and destroy it. For this reason, therefore, He said, "My God, My God, why hast Thou forsaken Me?" This word has besides an inward meaning, according to which Christ, in His sensitive parts, complained to His Father that He had been forsaken by Him. For as many as contend for His honour, and endure patiently the troubles of this world, our merciful God so moderates and tempers their crosses and afflictions by the inpouring of His divine consolation, that by His sensible grace He makes their crosses hardly felt; but He left His own beloved Son quite without any comfort, and so deprived Him of all consolation and light, that He endured as much in His human nature as had been ordained by the Eternal Wisdom, according to the strictness of justice, as much as was needed to atone for so many sins. And indeed our salvation was the more nobly and perfectly achieved, in that it was done and finished without any light at all, in absolute resignation and abandonment. For a chief cause of the Passion was to show clearly how great was the injury and insult brought upon His most high Godhead by the sins of the human race. Now as the knowledge of Christ was greater and more acute than that of all other beings, in heaven or in earth, so much the greater and heavier was His sorrow and agony. Nay more--what is more wonderful than anything--whatever afflictions have been endured by all the saints, as members of Christ, existed much more abundantly in Christ their Head; and this I wish to be understood according to the spirit and reasonably. For all the saints have suffered no more than flowed in upon them through Christ, joined to them as His members, who communicated to them His own afflictions. For He took upon Himself the afflictions of all the saints, out of His great love for His members, and wondrous pity, and He suffered far greater internal anguish than any of the saints, nay, more even than the blessed Virgin, His mother, felt her own sharp sorrow and sickness of heart. For if an earthly father loves his child so much, that in fatherly pity he takes upon himself the sorrows of his child, and grieves for them as if he suffered them himself, what must have been Christ's Cross and compassion for the affliction of His members, and above all, of those who suffered for His name's sake? Truly He bore witness to His members, how much He suffered from their afflictions, and how great was His inward pity for their sufferings, when He took all their debt upon Himself, and abolished all the penalties which they had merited, so that they might depart free. The same is most amply proved by the words which He spoke to St Paul, when He said, "Saul, Saul, why persecutest thou Me?" For the persecution which Saul had stirred up against the disciples, the members of the Lord, was not less grievous to Him than if He had suffered it Himself. Therefore He says to His friends and members, "He who touches you, touches the apple of Mine eye." For is there anything suffered by the members, which the Head does not suffer with them, He whose nature is goodness, and whose property is always to have mercy and to forgive?

THE FIFTH WORD

OUR most tender Lord was so worn out and parched by the extreme bitterness of His pain and suffering, and by the great loss of blood, that He cried, "I thirst." A little word, but full of mysteries.

In the first place it may be understood literally. For it is natural for those who are at the point of death to feel thirst, and to desire to drink. But how great was the drouth felt by Him who is the fountain of living water, but who was now worn out and parched by the heat of His ardent love, when he could truly say, "I am poured out like water," and "My strength is dried up like a potsherd." For not only did He shed all His own blood, and pour out moisture by tears, but the very marrow of His bones, and all His heart's blood, were consumed for our sakes by the heat and flame of love. Therefore He said rightly, "I thirst."

But, secondly, the word may be understood spiritually, as if Christ said to all men, "I thirst for your salvation." Hence St Bernard says: "Jesus cried, I thirst, not, I grieve. O Lord, what dost Thou thirst for? For your faith, your joy. I thirst because of the torments of your souls, far more than for My own bodily sufferings. Have pity on yourselves, if not on Me." And again, "O good Jesus, Thou wearest the crown of thorns; Thou art silent about Thy Cross and wounds, yet Thou criest out, I thirst. For what, then, dost Thou thirst? Truly, for the redemption of mankind only, and for the felicity of the human race." This thirst of Christ was a hundred times more keen and intense than His natural thirst. And, besides, He had another sort of thirst--that is to say, a thirst to suffer more, and to prove to us still more clearly His immeasurable love, as if He said to man, "See how I am worn out and exhausted for thy salvation. See how terrible are the pains and anguish which I endure. The fierce cruelty of man has almost brought Me to nothing; the sinners of earth have drunk out all My blood, and yet I thirst. Not yet is My heart satisfied, nor My desire accomplished, nor the fire of My love quenched. For if it were possible for Me, and according to My Father's will, that I should be crucified again a thousand times for your salvation and conversion, or that I should hang here, in all this pain and anguish, till the day of judgment, I would gladly do it, to prove to you the immeasurable love which I bear you in My heart, and to soften your stony hearts and rouse you to love Me in return. This is why I hang here so thirsty by the fountain of your hearts, that I may watch the pious souls who come hither to draw from the deep well of My Passion. Therefore, the maiden to whom I shall say, 'Give Me to drink a little water out of the pitcher of thy conscience'-- the water of devotion, pity, tears, and mutual love--and who shall let down to Me her pitcher, and shall say, 'Drink, my Lord; and for Thy camels also--that is, Thy servants, who carry Thee about daily on their bodies, and who by night and day are held bound fast by Thy yoke, I will draw the water of brotherly love'--that is the maiden whom the Lord hath prepared for the Son of My Lord, even the bride of the Word of God, united to My humanity. And she shall be counted worthy to enter, like a bride with her bridegroom, into the chamber of eternal rest, when the Bridegroom invites her, saying, 'Come, My blessed bride, inherit the Kingdom of My Father. For I was thirsty, and thou gavest Me drink.'"

Thirdly, we may apply this word to the Father, as if Christ said to His Father: "Father, I have declared Thy name to mankind; I have finished the work which Thou gavest Me to do; and in Thy service I have spent My whole body as Thine instrument. Behold, I am all worn out and exhausted; and yet I still thirst to do and suffer more for Thine honour. This is why I hang here, extended to the furthest breadth of love, for I long to be an everlasting sacrifice, a sweet savour to Thee, and at the same time an eternal atonement and salvation to mankind." Thus, too, might this strong Samson have said: "O Lord, Thou hast put into the hand of Thy servant this very great salvation and victory, and yet behold, I die of thirst." As if He would say: "Father, I have accomplished Thy gracious will; I have finished the work of man's salvation, as Thou didst demand; and yet I still thirst; for the sins by which Thou art offended are infinite. And so I desire that the love and merits of My Passion, by which Thou wilt be appeased, may be infinite too. And as I now offer myself as a peace-offering and a living sacrifice for the salvation of all men, so through Me may all men appease Thee, by offering Me to Thee as a peace-offering to Thine eternal glory, in memory of My Passion, and to make good all their shortcomings." O how acceptable to the Father must this desire of love have been! For what was this thirst but a sweet and pleasant refreshment to the Father, and at the same time the blessed renovation of mankind? Or what other language does this burning throat speak to us, save that of Christ's burning love, without measure and without limit, out of which He did all His works? This truly is the most noble sacrifice of our redemption, this is that peace-offering which will be offered even to the last day, by all good men, to the Holy Ghost, to the highest Father, in memory of the Son, to the eternal glory of the adorable Trinity, and to the fruit of salvation for mankind. Here, certainly, is the inexhaustible storehouse of our reconciliation, which never fails, for it is greater than all the debts of the world. This is that immeasurable love, which is higher than the heavens, for it has repaired the ruin of the angels; deeper than hell, for it has freed souls from hell; wider and broader than the earth, for it is without end and incomprehensible by any created understanding. O how keen and intense was this thirst of our Lord! For not only did He then say once, "I thirst," but even now He says in our hearts continually, "I thirst; woman, give me to drink." So great, so mighty, is that thirst, that He asks drink not only from the children of Israel, but from the Samaritans. To each one He complaineth of His thirst. But for what dost Thou thirst, O good Jesus? "My meat and drink," saith He, "is that men should do My Father's will. Now this is the will of My Father, even your sanctification and salvation, that you may sanctify your souls by walking in My precepts, by doing works of repentance, by adorning yourselves with all virtues, in order that, like a bride adorned for her husband, you may be worthy to be present at My supper in My Father's kingdom, and to sleep with Me as My elect bride, in the chamber of My Father's heart." O how Christ longs to bring all men thither! This is the meaning of His words: "Where I am there shall also My servant be"; and again: "Father, I will that they may be one even as We are one." O, how incomprehensible is this thirst of Christ! What toil and labour He endured for thirty and three years, for the sake of it! For this His very heart's blood was poured out. See what our tender Lord says to His Father: "The zeal of Thine house hath even eaten Me." Truly, He would have submitted to be crucified a thousand times, rather than allow one soul to perish through any fault of His. O how this inward thirst tormented Him, when He thought that He had done all that He could, and even a hundredfold more than He need have done, and yet that so few had turned to Him, and been won by Him. His whole body was now worn out; all His blood was shed; nothing remained for Him to do; and therefore He was constrained to confess, "It is finished"; and yet by all His labours, afflictions, and sufferings, He had brought no richer harvest to the Father than this. Truly, this was the most bitter of all His sorrows, that after so hard a battle His victory had not been more glorious, and that He returned a conqueror to His Father with so few spoils. Therefore, all those who do not refresh Him by performing His will, and doing all that is pleasing and honourable to Him, and withstanding all that reason tells them to be displeasing to Him, will one day hear Him say, "I was thirsty, and ye gave Me no drink. Depart, ye cursed, into everlasting fire."

Fourthly, there is yet another inward meaning of this word--namely, that Christ spoke it out of the love which inwardly draws Him towards all men, thus making known to us His ardent love, and opening His own heart, as a delightful couch, on which we may feed pleasantly, and inviting us to it, saying, "I thirst for you." For as the liquid which we drink is sent down pleasantly through the throat into the body, and so passes into the substance and nature of our body, so Christ out of the ardent thirst of His love, takes spiritual pleasure in drinking in all men into Himself, swallowing them, as it were, and incorporating them into Himself, and bringing them into the secret chamber of His loving heart. Therefore He says: "I, if I be lifted up from the earth, will draw all men unto Me"--all men, that is, who allow themselves to be drawn by Me, and submit to Me as obedient instruments, suffering Me to do with them according to My gracious will. But those who resist Him quench not His thirst, but give Him a bitter draught instead, even the deeds of their own self-will. These, when our Lord tasteth them, He straightway rejects.

THE SIXTH WORD

WHEN Christ had tasted the draught of vinegar and gall, He spoke the sixth word: "It is finished." Thereby He signified that by His Passion had been fulfilled all the prophecies, types, mysteries, scriptures, sacrifices, and promises, which had been predicted and written about Him. This is that true

Son of God, for whom the Father of heaven made ready a supper in the kingdom of His eternal blessedness; and He sent His servant--that is the human nature of Christ, coming in the form of a servant, to call them that were bidden to the wedding. For Christ, when He took human nature upon Him, was not only a servant but a servant of servants, and served all of us for thirty and three years with great toil and suffering. Indeed, He spent His whole life in bidding all men to His supper. It was for this that He preached, and wrought miracles, and travelled from place to place, and proclaimed that the kingdom of heaven was at hand, and that all should be prepared for it. But they would not come. And when the Father of the household heard this, He said to His Servant: "Compel them to come in, that My house may be filled." Then that Servant thought within Himself: "How shall I be able without violence to compel these men to come, that rebellion may be avoided and yet that their privilege and power of free will may remain unimpaired? For if I compel them to come by iron chains, and blows, and whips, I shall have asses and not men." Then He said to Himself: "I perceive that man is so constituted as to be prone to love. Therefore I will show him such love as shall pass all his understanding, love than which no other love can be greater. If man will observe this, he will be so caught in its toils, that he will not be able to escape its heat and flame, and will be constrained to turn to God, and love Him in return. For, turn where he will, he will always be met by the immeasurable benefits, the infinite goodness, and the wonderful love of God; and at the same time he will feel more and more compelled to return love for love, till he will be no more able to resist it, and will be gently constrained to follow." When this was done, Jesus Christ, this faithful and wise Servant, said to His Lord and Father, "It is finished. I have finished the work which Thou gavest Me to do. What more could I have done, and have not done it? I have no member left that is not weary and worn with toil and pain. My veins are dry, My blood is shed; My marrow is spent, My throat is hoarse with crying. Such love have I shown to man, that his heart cannot be human, cannot even be stony, or the heart of a brute beast, but must be quite devilish and desperate, if it be not moved by the thought of these things."

Moreover, this word of our Lord Jesus is a word of sorrow, not of joy. He spoke it not as if He had now escaped from all His suffering. No; when He said, "It is finished," He meant all that had been ordained and decreed by the eternal Truth for Him to suffer. Besides, all the sufferings which had been inflicted upon Him by degrees and singly, He now endures together with immeasurable anguish. Who can have such a heart of adamant as not to be moved by such torment as this? How short were the words which our Lord Jesus spoke on the Cross, yet how full of sacramental mysteries! Now were fulfilled the words of Exodus: "And all things were finished which belonged to the sacrifice of the Lord."

Moreover by this word our Lord declared the glorious victory of the Passion, and how the old enemy, the jealous serpent, was overcome and thrown down; for this was the cause for which He suffered. For this He had taken upon Himself the garment of human nature, that He might vanquish and confound the enemy, by the same weapons wherewith the enemy boasted that he had conquered man. This was the chief purpose of His Passion, and now He confesses that it is finished. O how wonderful are the mysteries, and the victories, included in this little but deep word: "It is finished!" All that the eternal Wisdom had decreed, all that strict justice had demanded for each man, all that love had asked for, all the promises made to the fathers, all the mysteries, types, ceremonies in Scripture, all that was meet and necessary for our redemption, all that was needed to wipe out our debts, all that must repair our negligences, all that was glorious and loving for the exhibition of this splendid love, all that we could desire, for our spiritual instruction--in a word, all that was good and fitting for the celebration of the glorious triumph of our redemption, all is included in that one word, "It is finished." What, then, remains for Him, but to finish and perfect His life in this glorious conflict; and, because nothing remains for Him to do, to commend His precious soul into His Father's hands, seeing that He has fought the good fight, and finished His course in all holiness? It is meet, then, that He should obtain the crown of glory which His heavenly Father will give Him on the day of His exaltation.

Lastly, by this word Christ offered up all His toil, sorrow, and affliction for all the elect, as the Apostle saith: "Who in the days of His flesh offered up prayer and supplications with strong crying and tears unto Him who was able to save Him from death, and was heard in that He feared. For if the blood of bulls and of goats and the ashes of a heifer, sprinkling the unclean, sanctifieth to the purifying of the flesh, how much more shall the blood of Christ, who through the eternal Spirit offered Himself without spot to God, purge our conscience from dead works to serve the living God?"

THE SEVENTH WORD

OUR Lord Jesus cried again with a loud voice, and said, "Father, into Thy hands I commend My Spirit." O all ye who love our Lord Jesus Christ, come, I beseech you, and let us watch, with all devotion and pity, His passing away. Let us see what must have been His sorrow and agony and torment, when His glorious soul was now at last forced to pass out of His worthy and most sacred body, in which for thirty and three years it had rested so sweetly, peacefully, joyfully, and holily, even as two lovers on one bed. How hard was it for them to be rent asunder, between whom no disagreement had ever arisen, no strife, or quarrel, or treachery. How unspeakably grievous was that Cross, when His sacred body was compelled to part with so faithful a friend, so gentle an occupant, so loving a teacher and master; and how great was the sorrow with which His glorious and pure soul was torn away from so faithful a servant, which had ever served obediently, never sparing any trouble, never shrinking from cold or heat or hunger or thirst; always enduring labour and sorrow in gentleness and patience. O how great was this affliction! For, as the philosopher says: "Of all terrible things death is the most terrible, on account of the natural and mutual affection, which is very great, between soul and body." How much greater must have been the anguish and sorrow, when the most holy soul and body of Christ were sundered, between which there had always been such wonderful harmony and love. Therefore, with inward pity and anxious sorrow, let us meditate on this sad parting; for the death of Christ is our life.

Let us meditate devoutly how His sacred body, the instrument of our salvation, was steeped in anguish, when all His members, as if to bid a last farewell, were bowing themselves down to die! Who can look without remorse and sorrow and pity upon the most gracious face of Christ, and behold how it is changed into the pallor and likeness of death; how tears still flow from His dimmed eyes; how His sacred head is bent; how all His members prove to us, by signs and motions, the love which they can no longer show by deeds. Let us pity Him, I pray you, for He is our own flesh and blood, and it is for our sins, not His own, that He is shamefully slain. O ye who up till now have passed by the Cross of Jesus with tepid or cold hearts, and whom all these torments and tears, and His blood shed like water, have not been able to soften; now at last let this loud voice, this terrible cry, rend and pierce your hearts through and through. Let that voice which shook the heaven and the earth and hell with fear, which rent the rocks and laid open ancient graves, now soften your stony hearts, and lay bare the old sepulchres of your conscience, full of dead men's bones--that is to say, of wicked deeds, and call again into life your departed spirits. For this is the voice which once cried: "Adam, where art thou; and what hast thou done?" This is the voice which brought Lazarus from Hades, saying, "Lazarus, come forth: arise from the grave of sin, and let them free thee from thy grave-clothes." Truly it was not so much the grievousness of His sufferings, as the greatness of our sins, which made our Lord utter this cry. He cried also, to show that He had the dominion over life and death, over the living and the dead. For though he was quite worn out, and destitute of strength, and though He had borne the bitter pangs of death so long, beyond the power of man, yet He would not allow Death to put forth its power against Him, until it pleased Him.

With a loud voice He cried, that earthly men, who care only for the things of earth, might quake with fear and trembling, and to cause them to meditate and see how naked and helpless the Lord of lords departed from this life. With a terrible voice He cried, to stir up all those who live in wantonness, and who have grown old in their defilement, and send forth a foul savour, like dead dogs, so that at last these miserable men may rise from their lusts and pleasures and sensual delights, and see how the Son of God, who was never strained with any spot of defilement, went forth to His Father; and with what toil and pain and anguish He departed from the light of day, and what He had to suffer before He reached his Father's Kingdom. He also cried with a loud voice, that He might inflame the lukewarm and slothful to devotion and love.

Moreover He cried with a loud voice as a sign of the glorious victory which He had gained, when after a single combat with His strong and cruel enemy, and having descended into the arena--the battlefield of this world--He had routed him on Mount Calvary and stripped him bare of his spoils. This victory, this glorious triumph, Christ proclaimed with a loud voice, and thus departing from the battlefield triumphant and victorious, He departed to the place of all delights, to the heart and breast of God, His Father, commending to it, as to a safe refuge, both Himself and all His own, with the words, "Father, into Thy hands I commend My Spirit."

We may learn from these words that the eternal Word, our Lord Jesus Christ, had been let down like a fishing-hook or great net, by the Father of heaven, into the great sea of this world, that He might catch not fish but men. Hear how He says: "My word, that goeth forth out of My mouth shall not return unto Me void, but shall execute that which I please, and shall prosper in the thing whereto I send it." And this net is drawn by the Father out of the salt sea, to the peaceful shore of His fatherly heart, full of the elect, of works of charity, of repentance, patience, humility, obedience, spiritual exercises, merits and virtues. For Christ drew unto Himself all the afflictions and good deeds of the good; just as St Paul says, "I live; yet not I, but Christ liveth in me." Even so, Christ lives in all the good, and all who have been willing and obedient instruments in the hands of Christ. In all such Christ lives and suffers and works. For whatever good there is in all men, is all God's work. Therefore Christ, feeling His Father drawing Him, gathered together in Himself in a wonderful manner all the elect with all their works, and commended them to His Father, saying, "My Father, these are Thine; these are the spoils which I have won by My conquest, by the sword of the Cross; these are the vessels which I have purchased with My precious blood; these are the fruits of My labours. Keep in Thine own name those whom Thou hast given Me. I pray not that Thou shouldest take them out of the world, but that Thou shouldest keep them from the evil." Thus did Christ commend Himself and all His own into His Father's hands. Come therefore, O faithful and devout soul, and contemplate with great earnestness the coming in and the going out of thy Lord Jesus; follow Him with love and longing, even to the chamber and bed of joy, which He has prepared for thee in thy Father's heart. Happy would he be, who could now be dissolved with Christ, and die with the thief, and hear from the lips of the Lord that comfortable word, "This day shalt thou be with Me in paradise." And though this is not granted to us, yet whatever we can here gain by labours and watchings and fastings and prayers, let us commend it all with Christ to the Father; let us pour it back again into the fountain, whence it flowed forth for us; and let nothing be left in us of empty self-satisfaction, no seeking after human praise or honour or reward. But whatever our God hath been willing to do in us, let us return it back into His own hands and say, "We are nothing of ourselves. It is He who made us, and not we ourselves. All good was made by Him, and without Him was not anything made. When therefore He taketh with Him what He made Himself, we are absolutely nothing."

Lastly, Christ commended His soul into His Father's hands, to show us how the souls of good and holy men mount up after Him to the bosom of the eternal Father, who must otherwise have gone down to hell; for it is He who has opened to us the way of life, and His sacred soul, by making the journey safe and free from danger, has been our guide into the kingdom of heaven.

SUSO

SUSO AND HIS SPIRITUAL DAUGHTER

AFTER this, certain very high thoughts arose in the mind of the servitor's spiritual daughter, concerning which she asked him whether she might put questions to him. He replied, Yea verily: since thou hast been led through the proper exercises, it is permitted to thy spiritual intelligence to enquire about high things. Ask then whatever thou wilt. She said: Tell me, father, what is God, and how He is both One and Three? The servitor replied, These be indeed high questions. As to the first, What is God, you must know that all the Doctors who ever lived cannot explain it, for He is above all sense and reason. Yet if a man is diligent, and does not relax his efforts, he gains some knowledge of God, though very far off. Yet in this knowledge of God consists our eternal life and man's supreme happiness. In this way, in former times, certain worthy philosophers searched for God, and especially that great thinker Aristotle, who tried to discover the Author of Nature from the order of nature and its course. He sought earnestly, and he was convinced from the well-ordered course of nature that there must of necessity be one Prince and Lord of the whole universe--He whom we call God. About this God and Lord we know this much, that He is an immortal Substance, eternal, without before or after, simple, bare, unchangeable, an incorporeal and essential Spirit, whose substance is life and energy, whose most penetrating intelligence knows all things in and by itself, whose essence in itself is an abyss of pleasures and joys, and who is to Himself, and to all who shall enjoy Him in a future life, a supernatural, ineffable, and most sweet happiness. The maiden, when she heard this, looked up, and said: These things are sweet to tell and sweet to hear, for they rouse the heart, and lift the spirit up far beyond itself. Therefore, father, tell me more about these things. The servitor said: The Divine Essence, about which we speak, is an intelligible or intellectual Substance of such a kind, that it cannot be seen in itself by mortal eyes; but it can be discerned in its effects, even as we recognise a fine artist by his works. As the Apostle teaches us, "The invisible things of God from the creation of the world are clearly seen, being understood by the things that are made." For the creatures are a kind of mirror, in which God shines. This knowledge is called speculation, by which we contemplate the great Architect of the world in His works. Come now, look upward and about thee, through all the quarters of the universe, and see how wide and high the beautiful heaven is, how swift its motion, and how marvellously its Creator has adorned it with the seven planets, and with the countless multitude of the twinkling stars. Consider what fruitfulness, what riches, the sun bestows upon the earth, when in summer it sheds abroad its rays unclouded! See how the leaves and grass shoot up, and the flowers smile, and the woods and plains resound with the sweet song of nightingales and other birds; how all the little animals, after being imprisoned by grim winter, come forth rejoicing, and pair; and how men and women, both old and young, rejoice and are merry. O Almighty God, if Thou art so lovable and so pleasant in Thy creatures, how happy and blessed, how full of all joy and beauty, must Thou be in Thyself? But further, my daughter, contemplate the elements themselves--Earth, Water, Air, and Fire, with all the wonderful things which they contain in infinite variety--men, beasts, birds, fishes, and sea-monsters. And all of these give praise and honour to the unfathomable immensity that is in Thee. Who is it, Lord, who preserves all these things, who nourishes them? It is Thou who providest for all, each in his own way, for great and small, rich and poor. Thou, O God, doest this; Thou alone art God indeed! Behold, my daughter, thou hast now found the God whom thou hast sought so long. Look up, then, with shining eyes, with radiant face and exulting heart, behold Him and embrace Him with the outstretched arms of thy soul and mind, and give thanks to Him as the one and supreme Lord of all creatures. By gazing on this mirror, there springs up speedily, in one of loving and pious disposition, an inward jubilation of the heart; for by this is meant a joy which no tongue can tell, though it pours with might through heart and soul. Alas, I now feel within me, that I must open for thee the closed mouth of my soul; and I am compelled, for the glory of God, to tell thee certain secrets, which I never yet told to any one. A certain Dominican, well known to me, at the beginning of his course used to receive from God twice every day, morning and evening, for ten years, an outpouring of grace like this, which lasted about as long as it would take to say the "Vigils of the Dead" twice over.[40] At these times he was so entirely absorbed in God, the eternal Wisdom, that he would not speak of it. Sometimes he would converse with God as with a friend, not with the mouth, but mentally; at other times he would utter piteous sighs to Him; at other times he would weep copiously, or smile silently. He often seemed to himself to be flying in the air, and swimming between time and eternity in the depth of the Divine wonders, which no man can fathom. And his heart became so full from this, that he would sometimes lay his hand upon it as it beat heavily, saying, "Alas, my heart, what labours will befall thee to-day?" One day it seemed to him that the heart of his heavenly Father was, in a spiritual and indescribable manner, pressed tenderly, and with nothing between, against his heart; and that the Father's heart--that is, the eternal Wisdom, spoke inwardly to his heart without forms.[41] Then he began to exclaim joyously in spiritual jubilation: Behold, now, Thou whom I most fervently love, thus do I lay bare my heart to Thee, and in simplicity and nakedness of all created things I embrace Thy formless Godhead! O God, most excellent of all friends! Earthly friends must needs endure to be distinct and separate from those whom they love; but Thou, O fathomless sweetness of all true love, meltest into the heart of Thy beloved, and pourest Thyself fully into the essence of his soul, that nothing of Thee remains outside, but Thou art joined and united most lovingly with Thy beloved.

To this the maiden replied: Truly it is a great grace, when anyone is thus caught up into God. But I should like to be informed, whether this is the most perfect kind of union or not? The servitor answered: No, it is not the most perfect, but a preliminary, gently drawing a man on, that he may arrive at an essential way of being carried up into God. The maiden asked him what he meant by essential and non-essential. He answered: I call that man essential or habitual (so to speak), who by the good and persevering practice of all the virtues, has arrived at the point of finding the practice of them in their highest perfection pleasant to him, even as the brightness of the sun remains constant in the sun. But I call him non-essential, in whom the brightness of the virtues shines in an unstable and imperfect way like the brightness of the moon. That full delight of grace which I described is so sweet to the spirit of the non-essential man, that he would be glad always to have it. When he has it, he rejoices; when he is deprived of it, he grieves inordinately; and when it smiles upon him, he is reluctant to pass to doing other things, even things that are pleasing to God; as I will show you by an example. The servitor of the Divine Wisdom was once walking in the chapter-house, and his heart was full of heavenly jubilation, when the porter called him out to see a woman who wished to confess to him. He was unwilling to interrupt his inward delight, and received the porter harshly, bidding him tell the woman that she must find some one else to confess to, for he did not wish to hear her confession just then. She, however, being oppressed with the burden of her sins, said that she felt specially drawn to seek comfort from him, and that she would confess to no one else. And when he still refused to go out, she began to weep most sadly, and going into a corner, lamented greatly. Meanwhile, God quickly withdrew from the servitor the delights of grace, and his heart became as hard as flint. And when he desired to know the cause of this, God answered him inwardly: Even as thou hast driven away uncomforted that poor woman, so have I withdrawn from thee my Divine comfort. The servitor groaned deeply and beat his breast, and hurried to the door, and as he did not find the woman there, was much distressed. The porter, however, looked about for her everywhere, and when he found her, still weeping, bade her return to the door. When she came, the servitor received her gently, and comforted her sorrowing heart. Then he went back from her to the chapter-house, and immediately God was with him, with His Divine consolations, as before.

Then said the maiden: It must be easy for him to bear sufferings, to whom God gives such jubilation and internal joys. And yet, said the servitor, all had to be paid for afterward with great suffering. However, at last, when all this had passed away, and God's appointed time had come, the same grace of jubilation was restored to him, and remained with him almost continuously both at home and abroad, in company and alone. Often in the bath or at table the same grace was with him; but it was now internal, and did show itself outside.

Then the maiden said: My father, I have now learned what God is; but I am also eager to know where He is. Thou shalt hear, said the servitor. The opinion of the theologians is that God is in no particular place, but that He is everywhere, and all in all. The same doctors say that we come to know a thing through its name. Now one doctor says that Being is the first name of God. Turn your eyes, therefore, to Being in its pure and naked simplicity, and take no notice of this or that substance which can be torn asunder into parts and separated; but consider Being in itself, unmixed with any Not-Being. Whatever is nothing, is the negation of what is; and what is, is the negation of what is not. A thing which has yet to be, or which once was, is not now in actual being. Moreover, we cannot know mixed being or not-being unless we take into account that which is all-being. This Being is not the being of this or that creature; for all particular being is mixed with something extraneous, whereby it can receive something new into itself. Therefore the nameless Divine Being must be in itself a Being that is all-being, and that sustains all particular things by its presence.

It shows the strange blindness of man's reason, that it cannot examine into that which it contemplates before everything, and without which it cannot perceive anything. Just as, when the eye is bent on noticing various colours, it does not observe the light which enables it to see all these objects, and even if it looks at the light it does not observe it; so it is with the eye of the soul. When it looks at this or that particular substance, it takes no heed of the being, which is everywhere one, absolute and simple, and by the virtue and goodness of which it can apprehend all other things. Hence the wise Aristotle says, that the eye of our intelligence, owing to its weakness, is affected towards that being which is itself the most manifest of all things, as the eye of a bat or owl is towards the bright rays of the sun. For particular substances distract and dazzle the mind, so that it cannot behold the Divine darkness, which is the clearest light.

Come now, open the eyes of thy mind, and gaze if thou canst, on Being in its naked and simple purity. You will perceive that it comes from no one, and has no before nor after, and that it cannot change, because it is simple Being. You will also observe that it is the most actual, the most present, and the most perfect of beings, with no defect or mutation, because it is absolutely one in its bare simplicity. This is so evident to an instructed intellect, that it cannot think otherwise. Since it is simple Being, it must be the first of beings, and without beginning or end, and because it is the first and everlasting and simple, it must be the most present. If you can understand this, you will have been guided far into the incomprehensible light of God's hidden truth. This pure and simple Being is altogether in all things, and altogether outside all things. Hence a certain doctor says: God is a circle, whose centre is everywhere, and His circumference nowhere.

When this had been said, the maiden answered: Blessed be God, I have been shown, as far as may be, both what God is, and where He is. But I should like also to be told how, if God is so absolutely simple, He can also be threefold.

The servitor answered: The more simple any being is in itself, the more manifold is it in its energy and operation. That which has nothing gives nothing, and that which has much can give much. I have already spoken of the inflowing and overflowing fount of good which God is in Himself. This infinite and superessential goodness constrains Him not to keep it all within Himself, but to communicate it freely both within and without Himself. But the highest and most perfect outpouring of the good must be within itself, and this can be nought else but a present, interior, personal and natural outpouring, necessary, yet without compulsion, infinite and perfect. Other communications, in temporal matters, draw their origin from this eternal communication of the Divine Goodness. Some theologians say that in the outflow of the creatures from their first origin there is a return in a circle of the end to the beginning; for as the emanation of the Persons from the Godhead is an image of the origin of the creatures, so also it is a type of the flowing back of the creatures into God. There is, however, a difference between the outpouring of the creatures and that of God. The creature is only a particular and partial substance, and its giving and communication is also partial and limited. When a human father begets a son, he gives him part, but not the whole, of his own substance, for he himself is only a partial good. But the outpouring of God is of a more interior and higher kind than the creature's outpouring, inasmuch as He Himself is a higher good. If the outpouring of God is to be worthy of His pre-eminent being, it must be according to personal relations.

Now, then, if you can look upon the pure goodness of the highest Good (which goodness is, by its nature, the active principle of the spontaneous love with which the highest Good loves itself) you will behold the most excellent and superessential outpouring of the Word from the Father, by which generation all things exist and are produced; and you will see also in the highest good, and the highest outpouring, the most holy Trinity, Father, Son, and Holy Ghost, existing in the Godhead. And if the highest outpouring proceeds from the highest essential good, it follows that there must be in this Trinity the highest and most intimate consubstantiality or community of being, and complete equality and identity of essence, which the Persons enjoy in sweetest communion, and also that the Substance and power of the three almighty Persons is undivided and unpartitioned.

Here the maiden exclaimed: Marvellous! I swim in the Godhead like an eagle in the air. The servitor, resuming his exposition, continued: It is impossible to express in words how the Trinity can subsist in the unity of one essence.

Nevertheless, to say what may be said on the subject, Augustine says that in the Godhead the Father is the Fountain-head of the Son and the Holy Ghost. Dionysius says, that in the Father there is an outflowing of the Godhead, which naturally communicates itself to the Word or Son. He also freely and lovingly pours Himself out into the Son; and the Son in turn pours Himself out freely and lovingly into the Father; and this love of the Father for the Son, and of the Son for the Father, is the Holy Ghost. This is truly said, but it is made clearer by that glorious Doctor of the Church, St Thomas, who says as follows: In the outpouring of the Word from the Father's heart, God the Father must contemplate Himself with His own mind, bending back, as it were, upon His Divine essence; for if the reason of the Father had not the Divine essence for its object, the Word so conceived would be a creature instead of God; which is false. But in the way described He is "God of God." Again, this looking back upon the Divine essence, which takes place in the mind of God, must, in a manner, produce a natural likeness; else the Word would not be the Son of God. So here we have the unity of essence in the diversity of Persons; and a clear proof of this distinction may be found in the word of that soaring eagle St John: "The Word was in the beginning with God."

Thus the Father is the Fountain-head of the Son, and the Son is the outflowing of the Father; and the Father and Son pour forth the Spirit; and the Unity, which is the essence of the Fountain-head, is also the substance of the three Persons. But as to how the Three are One, this cannot be expressed in words, on account of the simplicity of that Abyss. Into this intellectual Where, the spirits of men made perfect soar and plunge themselves, now flying over infinite heights, now swimming in unfathomed depths, marvelling at the high and wonderful mysteries of the Godhead. Nevertheless, the spirit remains a spirit, and retains its nature, while it enjoys the vision of the Divine Persons, and abstracted from all occupation with things below contemplates with fixed gaze those stupendous mysteries. For what can be more marvellous than that simple Unity, into which the Trinity of the Persons merges itself, and in which all multiplicity ceases? For the outflowing of the Persons is always tending back into the Unity of the same essence, and all creatures, according to their ideal existence in God, are from eternity in this Unity, and have their life, knowledge, and essence in the eternal God; as it is said in the Gospel: "That which was made, was Life in Him."[42] This bare Unity is a dark silence and tranquil inactivity, which none can understand unless he is illuminated by the Unity itself, unmixed with any evil. Out of this shines forth hidden truth, free from all falsehood; and this truth is born from the unveiling of the veiled Divine purity; for after the revelation of these things, the spirit is at last unclothed of the dusky light which up till now has followed it, and in which it has hitherto seen things in an earthly way. Indeed, the spirit finds itself now changed and something very different from what it supposed itself to be according to its earlier light: even as St Paul says, "I, yet not I." Thus it is unclothed and simplified in the simplicity of the Divine essence, which shines upon all things in simple stillness. In this modeless mode of contemplation, the permanent distinction of the Persons, viewed as separate, is lost. For, as some teach, it is not the Person of the Father, taken by Himself, which produces bliss, nor the Person of the Son, taken by Himself, nor the Person of the Holy Ghost, taken by Himself; but the three Persons, dwelling together in the unity of the essence, confer bliss. And this is the natural essence of the Persons, which by grace gives the substance or essence to all their creatures, and it contains in itself the ideas of all things in their simple essence. Now since this ideal light subsists as Being, so all things subsist in it according to their essential being, not according to their accidental forms; and since it shines upon all things, its property is to subsist as light. Hence all things shine forth in this essence in interior stillness, without altering its simplicity.

Then the maiden said: I could wish greatly, sir, that you could give me this mysterious teaching, as you understand it, under a figure, that I might understand it better. I should also be glad if you could sum up what you have been saying at length, so that it may stick more firmly in my weak mind. The servitor replied: Who can express in forms what has no form? Who can explain that which has no mode of being, and is above sense and reason? Any similitude must be infinitely more unlike than like the reality. Nevertheless, that I may drive out forms from your mind by forms, I will try to give you a picture of these ideas which surpass all forms, and to sum up a long discourse in a few words. A certain wise theologian says that God, in regard to His Godhead, is like a vast circle, of which the centre is everywhere, and the circumference nowhere. Now consider the image which follows. If anyone throws a great stone into the middle of a pool, a ring is formed in the water, and this ring makes a second ring, and the second a third; and the number and size of the rings depend on the force of the throw. They may even require a larger space than the limit of the pool. Suppose now that the first ring represents the omnipotent virtue of the Divine nature, which is infinite in God the Father. This produces another ring like itself, which is the Son. And the two produce the third, which is the Holy Ghost. The spiritual superessential begetting of the Divine Word is the cause of the creation of all spirits and all things. This supreme Spirit has so ennobled man, as to shed upon him a ray from His own eternal Godhead. This is the image of God in the mind, which is itself eternal. But many men turn away from this dignity of their nature, befouling the bright image of God in themselves, and turning to the bodily pleasures of this world. They pursue them greedily and devote themselves to them, till death unexpectedly stops them. But he who is wise, turns himself and elevates himself, with the help of the Divine spark in his soul, to that which is stable and eternal, whence he had his own origin: he says farewell to all the fleeting creatures, and clings to the eternal truth alone.

Attend also to what I say about the order in which the spirit ought to return to God. First of all, we should disentangle ourselves absolutely from the pleasures of the world, manfully turning our backs upon all vices; we should turn to God by continual prayers, by seclusion, and holy exercise, that the flesh may thus be subdued to the spirit. Next, we must offer ourselves willingly to endure all the troubles which may come upon us, from God, or from the creatures. Thirdly, we must impress upon ourselves the Passion of Christ crucified; we must fix upon our minds His sweet teaching, His most gentle conversation, His most pure life, which He gave us for our example, and so we must penetrate deeper and advance further in our imitation of Him. Fourthly, we must divest ourselves of external occupations, and establish ourselves in a tranquil stillness of soul by an energetic resignation, as if we were dead to self, and thought only of the honour of Christ and His heavenly Father. Lastly, we should be humble towards all men, whether friends or foes. . . . But all these images, with their interpretations, are as unlike the formless truth as a black Ethiopian is to the bright sun.

Soon after this holy maiden died, and passed away happy from earth, even as her whole life had been conspicuous only for her virtues. After her death she appeared to her spiritual father in a vision. She was clothed in raiment whiter than snow; she shone with dazzling brightness, and was full of heavenly joy. She came near to him, and showed him in what an excellent fashion she had passed away into the simple Godhead. He saw and heard her with exceeding delight, and the vision filled his soul with heavenly consolations. When he returned to himself, he sighed most deeply, and thus pondered: O Almighty God, how blessed is he, who strives after Thee alone! He may well be content to bear affliction, whose sufferings Thou wilt thus reward! May the Almighty God grant that we likewise may be brought to the same joys as this blessed maiden!

A MEDITATION ON THE PASSION OF CHRIST

THEN said the Eternal Wisdom to the servitor, Attend and listen dutifully, while I tell thee what sufferings I lovingly endured for thy sake.

After I had finished My last Supper with My disciples, when I had offered Myself to My enemies on the mount, and had resigned Myself to bear a terrible death, and knew that it was approaching very near, so great was the oppression of My tender heart and all My body, that I sweated blood; then I was wickedly arrested, bound, and carried away. On the same night they treated Me with insult and contumely, beating Me, spitting upon Me, and covering My head. Before Caiaphas was I unjustly accused and condemned to death. What misery it was to see My mother seized with unspeakable sorrow of heart, from the time when she beheld Me threatened with such great dangers, till the time when I was hung upon the cross. They brought Me before Pilate with every kind of ignominy, they accused Me falsely, they adjudged Me worthy of death. Before Herod I, the Eternal Wisdom, was mocked in a bright robe. My fair body was miserably torn and rent by cruel scourgings. They surrounded My sacred head with a crown of thorns; My gracious face was covered with blood and spittings. When they had thus condemned Me to death, they led Me out with My cross to bear the last shameful punishment. Their terrible and savage cries could be heard afar off: "Crucify, crucify, the wicked man."

Servitor. Alas, Lord, if so bitter were the beginnings of Thy passion, what will be the end thereof? In truth, if I saw a brute beast so treated in my presence I could hardly bear it. What grief then should I feel in heart and soul at Thy Passion? And yet there is one thing at which I marvel greatly. For I long, O my most dear God, to know only Thy Godhead; and Thou tellest me of Thy humanity. I long to taste Thy sweetness, and Thou showest me Thy bitterness. What meaneth this, O my Lord God?

Wisdom. No man can come to the height of My Godhead, nor attain to that unknown sweetness, unless he be first led through the bitterness of My humanity. My humanity is the road by which men must travel. My Passion is the gate, through which they must enter. Away then with thy cowardice of heart, and come to Me prepared for a hard campaign. For it is not right for the servant to live softly and delicately, while his Lord is fighting bravely. Come, I will now put on thee My own armour. And so thou must thyself also experience the whole of My Passion, so far as thy strength permits. Take, therefore, the heart of a man; for be sure that thou wilt have to endure many deaths, before thou canst put thy nature under the yoke. I will sprinkle thy garden of spices with red flowers. Many are the afflictions which will come upon thee; till thou hast finished thy sad journey of bearing the cross, and hast renounced thine own will and disengaged thyself so completely from all creatures, in all things, which might hinder thine eternal salvation, as to be like one about to die, and no longer mixed up with the affairs of this life.

Servitor. Hard and grievous to bear are the things which Thou sayest, Lord. I tremble all over. How can I bear all these things? Suffer me, O Lord, to ask Thee something. Couldst Thou not devise any other way of saving my soul, and of testifying Thy love towards me, so as to spare Thyself such hard sufferings, and so that I need not suffer so bitterly with Thee?

Wisdom. The unfathomable Abyss of My secret counsels no man ought to seek to penetrate, for no one can comprehend it. And yet that which thou hast suggested, and many other things, might have been possible, which nevertheless never happen. Be assured, however, that as created things now are, no more fitting method could be found. The Author of Nature doth not think so much what He is able to do in the world, as what is most fitting for every creature; and this is the principle of His operations. And by what other means could the secrets of God have been made known to man, than by the assumption of humanity by Christ? By what other means could he who had deprived himself of joy by the inordinate pursuit of pleasure, be brought back more fittingly to the joys of eternity? And who would be willing to tread the path, avoided by all, of a hard and despised life, if God had not trodden it Himself? If thou wert condemned to death, how could any one show his love and fidelity to thee more convincingly, or provoke thee to love him in return more powerfully, than by taking thy sentence upon himself? If, then, there is any one who is not roused and moved to love Me from his heart by My immense love, My infinite pity, My exalted divinity, My pure humanity, My brotherly fidelity, My sweet friendship, is there anything that could soften that stony heart?

Servitor. The light begins to dawn upon me, and I seem to myself to see clearly that it is as Thou sayest, and that whoever is not altogether blind must admit that this is the best and most fitting of all ways. And yet the imitation of Thee is grievous to a slothful and corruptible body.

Wisdom. Shrink not because thou must follow the footsteps of My Passion. For he who loves God, and is inwardly united to Him, finds the cross itself light and easy to bear, and has nought to complain of. No one receives from Me more marvellous sweetness, than he who shares My bitterest labours. He only complains of the bitterness of the rind, who has not tasted the sweetness of the kernel. He who relies on Me as his protector and helper may be considered to have accomplished a large part of his task.

Servitor. Lord, by these consoling words I am so much encouraged, that I seem to myself to be able to do and suffer all things through Thee. I pray Thee, then, that Thou wilt unfold the treasure of Thy Passion to me more fully.

Wisdom. When I was hung aloft and fastened to the wood of the cross (which I bore for My great love to thee and all mankind), all the wonted appearance of My body was piteously changed. My bright eyes lost their light; My sacred ears were filled with mocking and blasphemy; My sweet mouth was hurt by the bitter drink. Nowhere was there any rest or refreshment for Me. My sacred head hung down in pain; My fair neck was cruelly bruised; My shining face was disfigured by festering wounds; My fresh colour was turned to pallor. In a word, the beauty of My whole body was so marred, that I appeared like a leper--I, the Divine Wisdom, who am fairer than the sun.

Servitor. O brightest mirror of grace, which the Angels desire to look into, in which they delight to fix their gaze, would that I might behold Thy beloved countenance in the throes of death just long enough to water it with the tears of my heart, and to satisfy my mind with lamentations over it.

Wisdom. No one more truly testifies his grief over My Passion, than he who in very deed passes through it with Me. Far more pleasing to Me is a heart disentangled from the love of all transitory things, and earnestly intent on gaining the highest perfection according to the example which I have set before him in My life, than one which continually weeps over My Passion, shedding as many tears as all the raindrops that ever fell. For this was what I most desired and looked for in My endurance of that cruel death--namely, that mankind might imitate Me; and yet pious tears are very dear to Me.

Servitor. Since then, O most gracious God, the imitation of Thy most gentle life and most loving Passion is so pleasing to Thee, I will henceforth labour more diligently to follow Thy Passion than to weep over it. But since both are pleasing to Thee, teach me, I pray Thee, how I ought to conform myself to Thy Passion.

Wisdom. Forbid thyself the pleasure of curious and lax seeing and hearing; let love make sweet to thee those things which formerly thou shrankest from; eschew bodily pleasures; rest in Me alone; bear sweetly and moderately the ills that come from others; desire to despise thyself; break thy appetites; crush out all thy pleasures and desires. These are the first elements in the school of Wisdom, which are read in the volume of the book of My crucified body. But consider whether anyone, do what he may, can make himself for My sake such as I made Myself for his.

Servitor. Come then, my soul, collect thyself from all external things, into the tranquil silence of the inner man. Woe is me! My heavenly Father had adopted my soul to be His bride; but I fled far from Him. Alas, I have lost my Father, I have lost my Lover. Alas, alas, and woe is me! What have I done, what have I lost? Shame on me, I have lost myself, and all the society of my heavenly country. All that could delight and cheer me has utterly forsaken me; I am left naked. My false lovers were only deceivers. They have stripped me of all the good things which my one true Lover gave me; they have despoiled me of all honour, joy, and consolation. O ye red roses and white lilies, behold me a vile weed, and see also how soon those flowers wither and die, which this world plucks. And yet, O most gracious God, none of my sufferings are of any account, compared with this, that I have grieved the eyes of my heavenly Father. This is indeed hell, and a cross more intolerable than all other pain. O heart of mine, harder than flint or adamant, why dost thou not break for grief? Once I was called the bride of the eternal King, now I deserve not to be called the meanest of his handmaids. Never again shall I dare to raise mine eyes, for shame. O that I could hide myself in some vast forest, with none to see or hear me, till I had wept to my heart's desire. O Sin, Sin, whither hast thou brought me? O deceitful World, woe to those who serve thee! Now I have thy reward, I receive thy wages--namely, that I am a burden to myself and the whole world, and always shall be.

Wisdom. Thou must by no means despair; it was for thy sins and those of others that I came into this world, that I might restore thee to Thy heavenly Father, and bring thee back to greater glory and honour than thou ever hadst before.

Servitor. Ah, what is this, which whispers such flattering things to a soul that is dead, abhorred, rejected?

Wisdom. Dost thou not know Me? Why art thou so despondent? Art thou beside thyself with excessive grief, My dearest son? Knowest thou not that I am Wisdom, most gentle and tender, in whom is the Abyss of infinite mercy, never yet explored perfectly even by all the saints, but none the less open to thee and all other sorrowing hearts. I am he who for thy sake willed to be poor and an exile, that I might recall thee to thy former honour. I am He who bore a bitter death, that I might restore thee to life. I am thy Brother; I am thy Bridegroom. I have put away all the wrong that thou ever didst against Me, even as if it had never been, only henceforth, thou must turn wholly to Me, and never again forsake Me. Wash away thy stains in My blood. Lift up thy head, open thine eyes, and take heart. In token of reconciliation, take this ring and put it on thy finger as My bride, put on this robe, and these shoes on thy feet, and receive this sweet and loving name, that thou mayst both be and be called for ever My bride. Thou has cost Me much labour and pain; for that cause, the Abyss of My mercy toward thee is unfathomable.

Servitor. O kindest Father, O sweetest Brother, O only joy of my heart, wilt Thou be so favourable to my unworthy soul? What is this grace? What is the Abyss of Thy clemency and mercy? From the bottom of my heart I thank Thee, O heavenly Father, and beseech Thee by Thy beloved Son, whom Thou hast willed to suffer a cruel death for love, to forget my impieties. . . .

Now, O Lord, I remember that most loving word, wherewith in the book of Ecclesiasticus[43] Thou drawest us to Thyself. "Come to me, all ye who desire me, and be filled with my fruits. I am the mother of beautiful affection. My breath is sweeter than honey, and my inheritance above honey and the honeycomb." "Wine and music rejoice the heart, and above both is the love of Wisdom."[44] Of a surety, O Lord, Thou showest Thyself so lovable and desirable, that it is no wonder that the hearts of all long for Thee, and are tormented by the desire of Thee. Thy words breathe love, and flow so sweetly, that in many hearts the love of temporal things has wholly dried up. Therefore, I greatly long to hear Thee speak of Thy lovableness. Come, O Lord, my only comfort, speak to the heart of Thy servant. For I sleep sweetly beneath Thy shadow, and my heart is awake.

Wisdom. Hear, My son, and see; incline thine ear, forgetting thyself and all other things. Lo, I in Myself am that ineffable Good, which is and ever was; which has never been expressed nor ever will be. For although I give Myself to be felt by men in their inmost hearts, yet no tongue can ever declare or explain in words what I am. For verily all the beauty, grace, and adornment which can be conceived by thee or by others, exists in me far more excellently, more pleasantly, more copiously, than any one could say in words. I am the most loving Word of the Father, begotten from the pure substance of the Father, and wondrously pleasing am I to His loving eyes in the sweet and burning love of the Holy Spirit. I am the throne of happiness, the crown of souls: most bright are Mine eyes, most delicate My mouth, My cheeks are red and white, and all My appearance is full of grace and loveliness. All the heavenly host gaze upon Me with wonder and admiration; their eyes are ever fixed upon Me, their hearts rest in Me, their minds turn to Me and turn again. O thrice and four times happy is he, to whom it shall be given to celebrate this play of love amid heavenly joys at My side, holding My tender hands in happiest security, for ever and ever to all eternity. Only the word that proceeds out of My sweet mouth surpasses the melodies of all the angels, the sweet harmony of all harps, and musical instruments of every kind....

Servitor. There are three things, O Lord, at which I marvel greatly. The first is, that although Thou art in Thyself so exceedingly loving, yet towards sin Thou art a most severe judge and avenger. Alas, Thy face in wrath is too terrible; the words which Thou speakest in anger pierce the heart and soul like fire. O holy and adorable God, save me from Thy wrathful countenance, and defer not till the future life my punishment.

Wisdom. I am the unchangeable Good, remaining always the same. The reason why I do not appear always the same, is on account of those who do not behold Me in the same way. By nature I am friendly; yet none the less I punish vice severely, so that I deserve to be feared. From My friends I require a pure and filial fear, and a friendly love, that fear may ever restrain them from sin, and that love may join them to Me in unbroken loyalty.

Servitor. What Thou sayest pleases me, O Lord, and it is as I would have it. But there is another thing at which I greatly marvel--how it is that when the soul is faint from desire of the sweetness of Thy presence, Thou art wholly mute, and dost not utter a single word that can be heard. And who, O Lord, would not be grieved, when Thou showest Thyself so strange, so silent, to the soul that loves Thee above all things?

Wisdom. And yet all the creatures speak of Me.

Servitor. But that is by no means enough for the soul that loves.

Wisdom. Also every word that is uttered about Me is a message of My love; all the voices of holy Scripture that are written about Me are letters of love, sweet as honey. They are to be received as if I had written them Myself. Ought not this to satisfy thee?

Servitor. Nay but, O most holy God, dearest Friend of all to me, Thou knowest well that a heart which is on fire with love is not satisfied with anything that is not the Beloved himself, in whom is its only comfort. Even though all the tongues of all the angelic spirits were to speak to me, none the less would my unquenchable love continue to yearn and strive for the one thing which it desires. The soul that loves Thee would choose Thee rather than the kingdom of heaven. Pardon me, O Lord: it would become Thee to show more kindness to those who love Thee so ardently, who sigh and look up to Thee and say: Return, return! Who anxiously debate with themselves: alas, thinkest thou that thou hast offended Him? That He has deserted thee? Thinkest thou that He will ever restore thee His most sweet presence, that thou wilt ever again embrace Him with the arms of Thy heart, and press Him to thy breast, that all thy grief and trouble may vanish? All this, O Lord, Thou hearest and knowest, and yet Thou art silent.

Wisdom. Certainly I know all this, and I watch it with great pleasure. But I would have thee also answer a few questions, since thy wonder, though veiled, is so great. What is it which gives the greatest joy to the highest of all created spirits?

℥ ervitor. Ah, Lord, this question is beyond my range. I prithee, answer it Thyself.

Wisdom. I will do as thou desirest. The highest angelic spirit finds nothing more desirable or more delightful than to satisfy My will in all things; so much so, that if he knew that it would redound to My praise for him to root out nettles and tares, he would diligently fulfil this task in preference to all others.

Servitor. Of a truth, Lord, this answer of Thine touches me sharply. I perceive that it is Thy will that I should be resigned in the matter of receiving and feeling tokens of Thy love, and that I should seek Thy glory alone, in dryness and hardness as well as in sweetness.

Wisdom. No resignation is more perfect or more excellent, than to be resigned in dereliction.

℥ ervitor. And yet, O Lord, the pain is very grievous.

Wisdom. Wherein is virtue proved, if not in adversity? But be assured, that I often come, and try whether the door into My house is open, but find Myself repulsed. Many times I am received like a stranger, harshly treated, and then driven out of doors. Nay, I not only come to the soul that loves me, but tarry with her like a friend; but that is done so secretly, that none know it save those who live quite detached and separated from men, and observe My ways, and care only to please and satisfy My grace. For according to My Divinity I am purest Spirit, and I am received spiritually in pure spirits.

Servitor. So far as I understand, Lord God, Thou art a very secret Lover. How glad would I be if Thou wouldest give me some signs, by which I might know Thee to be truly present.

Wisdom. By no other way canst thou know the certainty of My presence better, than when I hide Myself from thee, and withdraw what is Mine from thy soul. Then at last thou knowest by experience what I am, and what thou art. Of a surety I am everlasting Good, without whom no one can have anything good. When therefore I impart that immense Good, which is Myself, generously and lovingly, and scatter it abroad, all things to which I communicate Myself are clothed with a certain goodness, by which My presence can be as easily inferred, as that of the Sun, the actual ball of which cannot be seen, by its rays. If therefore thou ever feelest My presence, enter into thyself, and learn how to separate the roses from the thorns, the flowers from the weeds.

Servitor. Lord, I do search, and I find within myself a great diversity. When I am deserted by Thee, my soul is like a sick man, whose taste is spoiled. Nothing pleases me, but all things disgust me. My body is torpid, my mind oppressed; within is dryness, without is sadness. All that I see or hear, however good in reality, is distasteful and hateful to me. I am easily led into sins; I am weak to resist my enemies; I am cold or lukewarm towards all good. Whoever comes to me, finds my house empty. For the House-Father is away, who knows how to counsel for the best, and to inspire the whole household. On the other hand, when the day-star arises in my inmost heart, all the pain quickly vanishes, all the darkness is dispelled, and a great brightness arises and shines forth. My heart laughs, my mind is exalted, my soul becomes cheerful, all things around me are blithe and merry; whatever is around me and within me is turned to Thy praise. That which before seemed hard, difficult, irksome, impossible, becomes suddenly easy and pleasant. To give myself to fasting, watching, and prayer, to suffer or abstain or avoid, in a word all the hardnesses of life seem when compared with Thy presence to have no irksomeness at all. My soul is bathed in radiance, truth, and sweetness, so that all its labours are forgotten. My heart delights itself in abundant sweet meditations, my tongue learns to speak of high things, my body is brisk and ready for any undertaking; whoever comes to ask my advice, takes back with him high counsels such as he desired to hear. In short, I seem to myself to have transcended the limits of time and space, and to be standing on the threshold of eternal bliss. But who, O Lord, can secure for me, that I may be long in this state? Alas, in a moment it is withdrawn from me; and for a long space again I am left as naked and destitute as if I had never experienced anything of the kind; till at last, after many and deep sighings of heart, it is restored to me. Is this Thou, O Lord, or rather I myself? Or what is it?

Wisdom. Of thyself thou hast nothing except faults and defects. Therefore that about which thou askest is I Myself, and this is the play of love.

Servitor. What is the play of love?

Wisdom. So long as the loved one is present with the lover, the lover knoweth not how dear the loved one is to him; it is only separation which can teach him that.

Servitor. It is a very grievous game. But tell me, Lord, are there any who in this life no longer experience these vicissitudes of Thy presence?

Wisdom. You will find very few indeed. For never to be deprived of My presence belongs not to temporal but to eternal life.

APHORISMS AND MAXIMS

ACT according to the truth in simplicity; and, whatever happens, do not help thyself; for he who helps himself too much will not be helped by the Truth.

God wishes not to deprive us of pleasure; but He wishes to give us pleasure in its totality--that is, all pleasure.

Wilt thou be of use to all creatures? Then turn thyself away from all creatures.

If a man cannot comprehend a thing, let him remain quiet, and it will comprehend him.

Say to the creatures, I will not be to thee what thou art to me.

The power of abstaining from things gives us more power than the possession of them would.

Some men one meets who have been inwardly drawn by God, but have not followed Him. The inner man and the outer man in these cases are widely at variance, and in this way many fail.

He who has attained to the purgation of his senses in God performs all the operations of the senses all the better.

He who finds the inward in the outward goes deeper than he who only finds the inward in the inward.

He is on the right road who contemplates under the forms of things their eternal essence.

It is well with a man who has died to self and begun to live in Christ.

RUYSBROEK

THE ADORNMENT OF THE SPIRITUAL NUPTIALS

BOOK I

PREFACE

"SEE the Bridegroom cometh: go forth to meet Him." St Matthew the evangelist wrote these words, and Christ said them to His disciples and to all men, in the Parable of the Ten Virgins. The Bridegroom is our Lord Jesus Christ, and human nature is the bride, whom God has made in His own image and likeness. He placed her at first in the most exalted, the most beautiful, the richest and most fertile place on earth--in paradise. He subjected to her all the creatures; He adorned her with graces; and He laid a prohibition upon her, in order that by obedience she might deserve to be established in an eternal union with her Bridegroom, and never more fall into any affliction, trouble, or guilt. Then came a deceiver--the infernal, envious foe, under the guise of a cunning serpent. He deceived the woman, and the two together deceived the man, who possessed the essence of human nature. So the enemy despoiled human nature, the bride of God, by his deceitful counsels, and she was driven into a strange country; poor and miserable, a prisoner and oppressed, persecuted by her enemies, as if she could never more return to her country and the grace of reconciliation. But when God saw that the time was come, and took pity on the sufferings of His beloved, He sent His only Son to earth, in a rich abode and a glorious temple--that is to say, in the body of the Virgin Mary. There he married His bride, our nature, and united it to His Person, by means of the pure blood of the noble Virgin. The priest who joined the Bride and Bridegroom was the Holy Spirit; the angel Gabriel announced the marriage, and the blessed Virgin gave her consent. So Christ, our faithful Bridegroom, united our nature to His, and visited us in a strange land, and taught us the manners of heaven and perfect fidelity. And He laboured and fought like a champion against our enemy, and He broke the prison and gained the victory, and His death slew our death, and His blood delivered us, and He set us free in baptism under the life-giving waters, and enriched us by His sacraments and gifts, that we might go forth, as He said, adorned with all virtues, and might meet Him in the abode of His glory, to enjoy Him throughout all eternity.

Now the Master of truth, Christ, saith: "See, the Bridegroom cometh, go forth to meet Him." In these words Jesus, our Lover, teaches us four things. In the first word He gives a command, for He says, "See." Those who remain blind, and those who resist this command are condemned without exception. In the next word He shows us what we shall see--that is to say, the coming of the Bridegroom, when He says, "The Bridegroom cometh." In the third place, He teaches us and commands us what we ought to do, when He says, "Go forth." In the fourth place, when He says, "to meet Him," He shows us the reward of all our works and of all our life, for that must be a loving "going forth," by which we meet our Bridegroom.

We shall explain and analyse these words in three ways, first, according to the ordinary mode of the beginner's life--that is to say, the active life, which is necessary to all who would be saved. In the second place, we shall analyse these words by applying them to the inner life, exalted and loving, to which many men arrive by the virtues and by the grace of God. Thirdly, we shall explain them by applying them to the superessential and contemplative life, to which few attain and which few can taste, because of the supreme sublimity of this life.

ON THE ACTIVE LIFE

CHRIST, the Wisdom of the Father, hath said from the time of Adam and still saith (inwardly, according to His Divinity), to all men, "See"; and this vision is necessary. Now let us observe attentively that for him who wishes to see materially or spiritually, three things are necessary. First, in order that a man may be able to see materially, he must have the external light of heaven, or another natural light, in order that the medium--that is to say, the air across which one sees, may be illuminated. In the second place, he must have the will, that the things which he will see may be reflected in his eyes. Thirdly, he must have the instruments, his eyes, healthy and without flaw, that the material objects may be exactly reflected in them. If a man lacks any one of these three things, his material vision disappears. We shall speak no more of this vision, but of another, spiritual and supernatural, wherein all our blessedness resides.

Three things are necessary for spiritual and supernatural vision. First, the light of the divine grace, then the free conversion of the will towards God, and lastly, a conscience pure from all mortal sin. Now observe: God being a God common to all, and His boundless love being common to all, He grants a double grace; both antecedent grace, and the grace by which one merits eternal life. All men, heathens and Jews, good and bad, have in common antecedent grace. In consequence of the common love of God towards all men, He has caused to be preached and published His name and the deliverance of human nature, even to the ends of the earth. He who wishes to be converted can be converted. For God wishes to save all men and to lose none. At the day of judgment none will be able to complain that enough was not done for him, if he had wished to be converted. So God is a common Light and Splendour which illumine heaven and earth, and men according to their merits and their needs. But though God is common, and though the sun shines on all trees, some trees remain without fruit, and others bear wild fruit useless to mankind. This is why we prune these trees and graft fertile branches upon them, that they may bear good fruit, sweet to taste and useful for men. The fertile branch which comes from the living paradise of the eternal kingdom, is the light of divine grace. No work can have savour, or be useful to man, unless it comes from this branch. This branch of divine grace, which makes man acceptable and by which we merit eternal life, is offered to all. But it is not grafted on all, for they will not purge away the wild branches of their trees--that is to say, unbelief or a perverse will, or disobedience to the commandments of God. But in order that this branch of divine grace may be planted in our soul, three things are necessary; the antecedent grace of God, the conversion of our free will, and the purification of the conscience. Antecedent grace touches all men; but all men do not attain to free conversion and purification of the conscience, and this is why the grace of God, by which they might merit eternal life, fails to touch them. The antecedent grace of God touches man from within or from without. From without, by sickness or loss of outward goods, of relations and friends, or by public shame; or perhaps a man is moved by preaching, or by the examples of saints and just men, by their words or works, till he comes to the knowledge of himself. This is how God touches us from without. Sometimes also a man is touched from within, by recalling the pains and sufferings of our Lord, and the good which God has done to him and to all men, or by the consideration of his sins, of the shortness of life, of the eternal pains of hell and the eternal joys of heaven, or because God has spared him in his sins and has waited for his conversion; or he observes the marvellous works of God in heaven, on earth, and in all creation. These are the works of antecedent divine grace, which touch man from within or from without, and in divers manners. And man has still a natural inclination towards God, proceeding from the spark of his soul or synteresis, [Footnote: See Introduction] and from the highest reason, which always desires the good and hates the evil. Now, in these three manners God touches every man according to his needs, so that the man is struck, warned, frightened, and stops to consider himself. All this is still antecedent grace and not merited; it thus prepares us to receive the other grace, by which we merit eternal life; when the mind is thus empty of bad wishes and bad deeds, warned, struck, in fear of what it ought to do, and considers God, and considers itself with its evil deeds. Thence come a natural sorrow for sin and a natural good will. This is the highest work of antecedent grace.

When man does what he can, and can go no further because of his weakness, it is the infinite goodness of God which must finish this work. Then comes a higher splendour of the grace of God, like a ray of the sun, and it is poured upon the soul, though it is as yet neither merited nor desired. In this light God gives Himself, by free will and by bounty, and no one can merit it before he has it. And it is in the soul an internal and mysterious operation of God, above time, and it moves the soul and all its faculties. Here then ends antecedent grace; and here begins the other--that is to say, supernatural light.

This light is the first necessary condition, and from it is born a second spiritual condition--that is to say, a free conversion of the will in a moment of time, and then love is born in the union of God and the soul. These two conditions are connected, so that one cannot be accomplished without the other. There, where God and the soul are united in the unity of love, God grants His light above time, and the soul freely turns to God by the force of grace, in a moment of time, and charity is born in the soul, from God and the soul, for charity is a bond of love between God and the loving soul. From these two things, the grace of God, and the free conversion of the will illuminated by grace, is born charity--that is to say, divine love. And from divine love proceeds the third point, the purification of the conscience. And this is accomplished in the consideration of sin and of the flaws in the soul, and because man loves God, there enters into him a contempt for self and for all his works. This is the order of conversion. From it are born a true repentance and a perfect sorrow for the evil that we have done, and an ardent desire to sin no more and to serve God henceforward in humble obedience; from it are born a sincere confession, without reserves, without duplicity and without pretences, the desire to satisfy God and to undertake the practice of all the virtues and all good works. These three things, as you have just heard, are necessary for divine vision. If you possess them, Christ says to you, "See," and you become really seeing. This is the first of the four chief ways in which Christ, our Lord, says "See."

ON THE FIRST COMING OF CHRIST, IN THE FLESH

NEXT, He shows us what we shall see when He says, "The Bridegroom cometh." Christ, our Bridegroom, says this word in Latin: Venit. The word expresses two tenses, the past and the present, and yet here it indicates the future. And this is why we must consider three comings of our Bridegroom Jesus Christ. At His first coming He was made man for love of man. The second coming is daily and frequent in every loving soul, with new graces and new gifts, as man is able to receive them. In the third coming, He will come manifestly on the dreadful day of judgment or at the hour of each man's death. In all these comings we must observe three things, the cause, the interior mode, and the external work.

The cause of the creation of angels and men is the infinite goodness and nobleness of God; He wished that the wealth and blessedness, which are Himself, should be revealed to reasonable creatures, for them to enjoy in time, and in eternity above time. The reason why God became man, is His inconceivable love, and the distress of all men, lost since the fall in original sin, and unable to raise themselves again. But the reason why Christ, according to His divinity and His humanity, accomplished His works on earth, is fourfold-- namely, His divine love, which is without measure; the created love, which is called charity, and which He had in His soul by the union of the Eternal Word and the perfect gift of His Father; the great distress of human nature; and the glory of His Father. These are the reasons for the coming of Christ, our Bridegroom, and for all His works, exterior and interior.

Now we must observe in Jesus Christ, if we wish to follow Him in His virtues according to our powers, the mode or condition which He had within, and the works which He wrought without, for they are virtues and the acts of virtues.

The mode which He had according to His divinity is inaccessible and incomprehensible to us, for it is after this mode that He is continually born of the Father, and that the Father in Him and by Him knows and creates and orders, and rules everything in heaven and on earth; for He is the Wisdom of the Father, and from them flows spiritually a Spirit--that is to say, a love, which is the bond between them and the bond of all the saints and just persons on earth and in heaven. We will speak no more of this mode but of the created mode which He had by these divine gifts and according to His humanity. These modes are singularly multiform; for Christ had as many modes as He had interior virtues, for each virtue has its special mode. These virtues and these modes were, in the mind of Christ, above the intelligence and above the comprehension of all creatures. But let us take three--namely, humility, charity, and interior or exterior suffering in patience. These are the three principal roots and origins of all virtues and all perfection.

ON THE TWOFOLD HUMILITY OF CHRIST

NOW understand: there are two kinds of humility in Jesus Christ, according to His divinity. First, He willed to become man; and this nature, which was accursed even to the depth of hell, He accepted according to His personality and was willing to unite Himself to it. So that every man, good or bad, may say, Jesus Christ, the Son of God, is my brother. Secondly, He chose for mother a poor virgin, and not a king's daughter, so that this poor virgin became the mother of God, who is the only Lord of heaven and earth and all creatures. In consequence, of all the works of humility which Christ ever accomplished, one may say that God accomplished them. Now let us take the humility which was in Jesus Christ according to His humanity and by grace and divine gifts; according to His humility His soul inclined with all its power in respect and veneration before the power of the Father. For an inclined heart is a humble heart. This is why He did all His works to the praise and glory of the Father, and sought in nothing His own glory according to His humanity. He was humble, and submitted to the old law, and to the commandments, and often to the customs. He was circumcised, and carried to the Temple, and redeemed according to usages, and He paid taxes to Caesar like other Jews. And He submitted Himself humbly to His mother and to Joseph, and served them with a sincere deference according to their needs. He chose for friends--for apostles--the poor and the despised, in order to convert the world. In his intercourse with them and all others He was humble and modest. This is why He was at the disposal of all men, in whatever distress they were, within or without; He was, as it were, the servant of the whole world. This is what we find first in Jesus Christ, our Bridegroom.

ON THE LOVE OF CHRIST, ADORNED WITH ALL VIRTUES

NEXT comes charity, the beginning and source of all virtues. This charity maintained the supreme forces of His soul in tranquillity, and in the enjoyment of the same blessedness which He enjoys at present. And this same charity kept Him continually exalted towards His Father, with veneration, love, praise, respect, with internal prayers for the need of all men, and with the offering of all His works to the glory of God the Father. And this same charity made Christ still overflow with love and kindness towards all the material or spiritual needs of mankind. This is why He has given, by His life, the model after which all men should fashion their lives. He has given spiritual nourishment to all well-disposed men by real internal teachings, as well as by outward miracles. We cannot comprehend His charity to its full extent, for it flowed from the unfathomable fountains of the Holy Spirit, above all the creatures who have ever received charity, for He was God and man in one Person. This is the second point of charity.

ON THE PATIENCE OF CHRIST, EVEN UNTO DEATH

THE third point is to suffer in patience. We will examine this seriously, for it is this which adorned Christ, our Bridegroom, during all His life. He suffered when He was newly born, from poverty and cold. He was circumcised and shed his blood. He was obliged to fly into a foreign country. He served Joseph and His mother, He suffered from hunger and thirst, from shame and contempt and from the wicked words and deeds of the Jews. He fasted, He watched, and was tempted by the enemy. He was subject to all men, He went from district to district, from town to town, to preach the gospel painfully and zealously. Finally, He was taken by the Jews, who were His enemies and whom He loved. He was betrayed, mocked, insulted, scourged, struck, and condemned on false testimony. He carried His cross with great pain to the mount of Calvary. He was stripped naked as at His birth, and never was seen a body so beautiful, nor a mother so unhappy. He endured shame, pain, and cold before all the world, for He was naked, and it was cold, and He was exhausted by His wounds. He was nailed with large nails to the wood of the cross, and was so strained that His veins were burst. He was lifted up and shaken upon the cross, so as to make His wounds bleed, His head was crowned with thorns, and His ears heard the fierce Jews crying out, "Crucify Him! crucify Him!" and many other shameful words. His eyes saw the obstinacy and wickedness of the Jews, and the distress of His mother, and His eyes were extinguished under the bitterness of pain and death. His mouth and palate were hurt by the vinegar and gall, and all the sensitive parts of His body wounded by the scourge.

Behold then Christ, our Bridegroom, wounded to death, abandoned by God and the creatures, dying on the cross, hanging from a post, with no one to care much for Him except Mary, His unhappy mother, who nevertheless could not aid Him. And Christ suffered moreover spiritually, in His soul, from the hardness of the Jews' hearts and those who made Him die, for in spite of the prodigies and miracles which they saw, they remained in their wickedness; and He suffered by reason of their corruption and the vengeance which God was about to inflict upon them, in body and soul, for His death. He suffered moreover for the grief and misery of His mother and disciples, who were in great sadness. And He suffered because His death would be wasted for many men, and for the ingratitude of many, and for the blasphemies of those who would curse Him who died for love of us. And His nature and interior reason suffered because God withdrew from them the inflow of His gifts and consolations, and abandoned them to themselves in such distress. Therefore Christ complained and said, My God, my God, why hast Thou forsaken me?

Behold then the interior virtues of Christ; humility, charity, and suffering in patience. These three virtues Jesus, our Bridegroom, practised throughout His life, and He died in them, and He paid our debt by satisfying justice, and opened His side in His bounty. And thence flow rivers of delight, and sacraments of blessedness. And He was exalted to His power, and sat at the right hand of the Father, and reigns eternally. This is the first coming of our Bridegroom, and it is completely past.

ON THE SECOND COMING OF CHRIST, HOW HE EVERY DAY FLOWS INTO OUR HEARTS WITH NEW GRACE

THE second coming of Christ, our Bridegroom, takes place every day in just men. We do not wish to speak here of the first conversion of man, nor of the first grace which was given him when he was converted from sin to virtue. But we wish to speak of a daily increase of new gifts and new virtues, and of a more actual coming of Christ, our Bridegroom, into our soul. Now we must observe the cause, the mode, and the work, of this coming. The cause is fourfold; the mercy of God, our misery, the divine generosity, and our desire. These four causes make the virtues grow and increase.

Now understand. When the sun sends forth its bright rays into a deep valley between two high mountains, and while it is at the zenith, so that it can illuminate the depths of the valley, a triple phenomenon occurs; for the valley is lighted from the mountains, and it becomes warmer and more fertile than the plain. In the same way, when a just man sinks in his misery, and recognises that he has nothing, and is nothing, that he can neither halt nor go forward by his own strength; and when he perceives also that he fails often in virtues and good works, he thus confesses his poverty and distress, and forms the valley of humility. And because he is humble and in need, and because he confesses his need, he makes his plaint to the kindness and mercy of God. He is conscious of the sublimity of God, and of his own abasement.

Thus he becomes a deep valley. And Christ is the sun of justice and mercy, which burns at the meridian of the firmament--that is to say, at the right hand of the Father, and shines even to the bottom of humble hearts; for Christ is always moved by distress, when man humbly offers to Him complaints and prayers. Then the two mountains rise--that is to say, a double desire, in the first place a desire to serve and love God by his merits, in the second place to obtain excellent virtues. These two desires are higher than heaven, for they touch God without any intermediary, and desire His immense generosity. Then that generosity cannot be kept back, it must flow, for the soul is at this moment susceptible of receiving countless boons.

These are the causes of the second coming of Christ, with new virtues. Then the valley--that is to say, the humble heart, receives three things. It is enlightened the more, and illuminated by grace, and warmed by charity, and becomes more fertile in virtues and good works. Thus you have the cause, the mode, and the work, of this coming.

HOW WE MAY MAKE DAILY PROGRESS BY THE SACRAMENTS OF THE CHURCH

THERE is yet another coming of Christ, our Bridegroom, which takes place every day, in the growth of grace and in new gifts--that is to say, when a man receives some sacrament with a humble and well-prepared heart. He receives then new gifts and more ample graces, by reason of his humility, and by the internal and secret work of Christ in the sacrament. That which is contrary to the sacrament is in baptism the want of faith, in confession the want of contrition; it is to go to the sacrament of the altar in a state of mortal sin, or of bad will; and it is the same with the other sacraments.

ON THE THIRD COMING OF CHRIST, TO JUDGMENT

THE third coming, which is still future, will take place at the last judgment or at the hour of death. Christ, our Bridegroom and our Judge at this judgment, will recompense and avenge according to justice, for He will award to each according to his deserts. He gives to every just man, for every good work done in the spirit of the Lord, a reward without measure, which no creature can merit-- namely, Himself. But as He co-operates in the creature, the creature deserves, through His merit, to have a reward. And by a necessary justice He gives eternal pains to those who have rejected an eternal good for a perishable.

ON THE THIRD SPIRITUAL GOING FORTH, TO ALL THE VIRTUES

NOW understand and observe. Christ says at the beginning of our text, "See"--that is to say, see by charity and pureness of conscience, as you have been told. Now, He has shown us what we shall see--namely, His three comings.

He orders us what we must do next, and says, "Go forth" if you have fulfilled the first necessary condition--that is to say, if you see in grace and in charity, and if you have well observed your model, Christ, in His "going forth"; there leaps up in you, from your love and loving observation of your Bridegroom, an ardour of justice-- that is to say, a desire to follow Him in virtue. Then Christ says in you, "Go forth." This going forth must have three modes. We must go forth towards God, towards ourselves, and towards our neighbour by charity and justice; for charity always pushes upward, towards the kingdom of God, which is God Himself; for He is the source from which it flowed without any intermediary, and He remains always immanent in it. The justice which is born of charity wishes to perfect the manners and the virtues which are suitable to the kingdom of God--that is to say, to the soul. These two things, charity and justice, establish a solid foundation in the kingdom of the soul where God may dwell, and this foundation is humility. These three virtues support all the weight and all the edifice of all the virtues and all sublimity; for charity maintains man in presence of the unfathomable good things of God from whence it flows, so that it perseveres in God, and increases in all the virtues and in true humility; and justice maintains man in presence of the eternal truth of God, so that truth may be discovered by him, and that he may be illuminated, and may accomplish all the virtues without error. But humility maintains man always before the supreme power of God, so that he remains always abased and little, and abandons himself to God, and holds no longer by himself. This is the way in which a man must bear himself before God, that he may grow alway in new virtues.

HOW HUMILITY IS THE FOUNDATION OF ALL THE VIRTUES

NOW understand; for having made humility the base of everything, we must speak first of it. Humility is the desire of abasement or of depth--that is to say, an inclination or internal desire for abasement of heart and conscience before the sublimity of God. The justice of God exacts this submission, and, thanks to charity, the loving heart cannot abandon it. When the loving and humble man considers that God has served him so humbly, so lovingly, and so faithfully, and then that God is so high, so powerful, and so noble, and that man is so poor, little, and base, there is born from all this, in the humble heart, an immense respect and reverence towards God; for to reverence God in all works, within and without, is the first and most delightful work of humility, the sweetest work of charity, and the most suitable work of justice. For the humble and loving heart cannot pay honours to God and His noble humanity, nor abase himself so deeply as to satisfy his desire. That is why it seems to the humble man that he always does too little in honour of God and in his humble service. And he is humble, and venerates Holy Church and the sacraments, and he is temperate in meat and drink, in his words, and in all relations of life. He is content with poor raiment, with menial employment, and his face is naturally humble, without pretence. And he is hunible in his practices, within and without, before God and before men, that none may be offended by reason of him. Thus he tames and removes far from him all pride, which is the cause and origin of all sins. Humility breaks the snares of sin, the world, and the Devil. And man is ordered within himself, and established in the very place of virtue. Heaven is open to him, and God is inclined to hear his prayer, and he is loaded with graces. And Christ, the solid stone, is his support, and he who builds his virtues upon humility cannot go wrong.

ON OBEDIENCE

FROM this humility is born obedience, for only the humble man can be inwardly obedient. Obedience is a submission and pliant disposition, and a good will ready for all that is good. Obedience subjects a man to orders, to prohibitions, and to the will of God, and it subjects the soul and sensual force to the highest reason, in such a way that the man lives suitably and reasonably. And it makes men submissive and obedient to Holy Church and to the sacraments, and to all the good practices of holy Christianity. It prepares man, and makes him ready for the service of all, in works, in bodily and spiritual care, according to the needs of each, and prudence. Also, it drives far away disobedience, which is the daughter of pride, and which we ought to flee from more than from poison. Obedience in will and work adorns, extends, and manifests the humility of man. It gives peace to cloisters, and if it exists in the prelate, as it ought to exist, it attracts those who are under his orders. It maintains peace and equality among equals. And he who observes it is beloved by those who are above him, and the gifts of God, which are eternal, elevate and enrich him.

ON THE ABDICATION OF OUR OWN WILL

FROM this obedience is born the abdication of our own will. By this abdication the substance and occasion of pride are repulsed, and the greatest humility is accomplished. And God rules the man as He wills; and the will of the man is so well united to that of God that he can neither wish nor desire anything otherwise. He has put off the old man, and has put on the new man, renewed and perfect according to the divine will. It is of such an one that Christ said, "Blessed are the poor in spirit," that is, those who have renounced their will--"for theirs is the kingdom of heaven."

ON PATIENCE

FROM the abandonment of the will is born patience; for no one can be perfectly patient in everything, except he who has submitted his will to the will of God, and to all men in things useful and convenient. Patience is a tranquil endurance of all that can happen to a man, whether sent by God or by men. Nothing can trouble the patient man, neither the loss of earthly goods, nor the loss of friends or relations, nor sickness, nor disgrace, nor life, nor death, nor purgatory, nor the devil, nor hell. For he has abandoned himself to the will of God in true love. And, provided that mortal sin does not touch him, all that God orders for him in time or eternity seems light. This patience adorns a man, and arms him against anger and sudden rage, and against impatience of suffering, which often deceives a man within and without, and exposes him to manifold temptations.

ON GENTLENESS

FROM this patience are born gentleness and kindness, for no one can be gentle under adversity if not the patient man. Gentleness creates in man peace and repose from everything; for the gentle man endures insulting words and gestures, and bad faces and bad deeds, and all manner of injustice towards his friends and himself, and he is content with all, for gentleness is suffering in repose. Thanks to gentleness, the force of anger remains immovable in its tranquillity, the force of desire lifts itself up towards the virtues, and the reason rejoices, and the conscience dwells in peace, for the other mortal sins, such as anger and rage, are removed far from her. For the Spirit of God reposes in a gentle and humble heart, as Christ saith, "Blessed are the meek, for they shall inherit the earth"--that is to say, their own nature and the things of earth in meekness, and, after this life, the things of eternity.

ON KINDNESS

FROM the same source as gentleness comes kindness, for the gentle spirit alone can possess kindness. This kindness causes a man to oppose a loving face and friendly words, and all the works of pity, to those who are angry with him, and he hopes that they will return to themselves and amend. Thanks to mercy and kindness, charity remains lively and fruitful in a man; for the heart full of kindness is like a lamp full of precious oil; and the oil of kindness lightens the wandering sinner by its good example, and soothes and heals by consoling words and deeds those whose heart is wounded, saddened, or irritated. And it inflames and illumines those who are in charity, and no jealousy or envy can touch it.

ON COMPASSION

FROM kindness is born compassion, by which we sympathise with every one, for no one can suffer with all men, except he who has kindness. Compassion is an inward movement of the heart, aroused by pity for the bodily or spiritual distress of all men. This compassion makes a man partaker in Christ's sufferings, when he considers the reason of these sufferings, the resignation and love of Christ, His wounds, His tortures, His shame, His nobleness, His misery, the shame which He endured, the crown, the nails, and the death in patience. These unheard of and manifold pains of Christ, our Redeemer and Bridegroom, move to pity anyone who is capable of feeling pity. Compassion makes a man observe and note his faults, his want of power to do any good thing, and weakness in all that pertains to the glory of God; his lukewarmness and slowness, the multitude of his faults, the waste of his time, and his positive shortcomings in virtue and good conduct. All this makes a man truly sorry for himself. Then his compassion for himself makes him consider his errors and wanderings, the small care which he has of God and of his eternal salvation, his ingratitude for all the good that God has done him, and for all that He has suffered for man. And he considers also that he is a stranger to the virtues, that he neither knows them nor practises them, while he is clever and crafty in all that is bad and unjust; he sees how attentive he is to the loss or gain of worldly goods, how inattentive and indifferent towards God, the things of eternity, and his own salvation. This consideration makes the just man feel a great compassion towards the salvation of all men. The man will also observe with pity the bodily needs of his neighbour and the manifold pains of nature, when he sees the hunger which men suffer, the thirst, cold, nakedness, poverty, contempt, and oppression; the sadness which they feel at the loss of relations, friends, goods, honour, and repose; and the innumerable afflictions to which flesh is heir. All this rouses the just man to compassion, and he suffers with all men; but his greatest suffering arises when he sees the impatience of others under their own sufferings, by which they lose their reward and often deserve hell. This is the work of compassion and pity.

This work of compassion and love for all men overcomes and removes the third mortal sin--namely, hatred and envy; for compassion is a wound of the heart, which makes us love all men, and can only work healing in so far as some suffering lives in men; for God has ordained that mourning and pain must precede all the other virtues. This is why Christ said, "Blessed are they that mourn, for they shall be comforted"--that is to say, when they shall reap in joy what they now sow in compassion and sorrow.

ON GENEROSITY

FROM this compassion is born generosity, for no one can be supernaturally generous, with faith in all men, and with love, except the merciful man; though one many give to a particular individual without charity, and without supernatural generosity.

Generosity is the copious outflow of a heart moved with charity and pity. When a man considers with compassion the sufferings and pains of Christ, from this compassion is born generosity, which excites us to praise and thank Christ for His pains and for His love, at the same time that it causes to be born in us respect and veneration, and a joyous and humble submission of heart and soul, in time and in eternity. When a man observes and pities himself, and considers the good that God has done to him and his own weakness, he cannot help flowing out into the liberality of God, taking refuge in His pity and fidelity, and abandoning himself to God, with a free and perfect wish to serve Him for ever. The generous man, who observes the errors, the wanderings, and the injustice of men, desires and implores the outflow of the divine gifts and the exercise of their generosity on all men, that they may return to themselves and be converted to the truth. The generous man considers also with compassion the material needs of all men; he helps them, gives, lends, consoles to the best of his power. By means of this generosity, men practise the seven works of mercy, the rich by their services and the bestowal of their goods, the poor by good will and the desire to do good if they can, and thus the virtue of generosity is perfected. Generosity in the depth of the heart multiplies all the virtues, and illuminates the forces of the soul. For the generous, man is always of joyful spirit, he is without anxiety; he is full of sympathy, and is ready to do kindnesses to all men in the works of virtue. He who is generous, and loves not the things of earth, however poor he may be, is like unto God, for all that he has, and all the thoughts of his heart flow out of him in largess. And so he is delivered from the fourth of the deadly sins, avarice. Jesus Christ saith to these: "Blessed are the merciful, for they shall obtain mercy"; in the day when they shall hear this word spoken unto them: "Come, ye blessed of my Father, inherit the kingdom prepared for you from the foundation of the world."

ON ZEAL AND DILIGENCE

FROM this generosity are born supernatural zeal and diligence in all the virtues. None can exhibit this zeal, save the generous and diligent man. This is an internal and eager impulse towards all the virtues, and towards the imitation of Christ and the saints. In this zeal, a man desires to expend in the honour of God the united powers of his heart and senses, his soul and body, all that he is, and all that he may receive. This zeal makes a man watchful in reason and discrimination, and makes him practise the virtues in justice. Thanks to this supernatural zeal, all the forces of his soul are open to God, and prepared for all the virtues. His conscience is refreshed, and divine grace is increased, virtue is practised with joy, and his external works are adorned. He who has received this lively zeal from God is removed far from the fifth deadly sin-- lukewarmness and gloominess towards the virtues necessary for salvation. [Footnote: The best account in English of the deadly sin of acedia, too much neglected in modern religious teaching, is to be found in Bishop Paget's Spirit of Discipline.] And sometimes this lively zeal disperses heaviness and sluggishness of the bodily temperament. It is on this subject that Jesus Christ says: "Blessed are they who hunger and thirst after righteousness, for they shall be filled." This will be, when the glory of God shall be manifested, and shall fill every man in proportion to his love and justice.

ON TEMPERANCE AND SOBRIETY

FROM zeal are born temperance and sobriety within and without; for none can maintain true moderation in sobriety, if he is not thoroughly diligent and zealous to preserve his body and soul in justice. Sobriety separates the higher faculties from the animal faculties, and preserves a man from excesses. Sobriety wishes not to taste nor know those things which are not permitted.

The incomprehensible and sublime nature of God surpasses all the creatures in heaven and earth, for whatever the creature conceives is creature. But God is above every creature, and within and without every creature, and all created comprehension is too strait to comprehend Him. In order that the creature may conceive and comprehend God, it must be drawn up into God from above; it is only by God that it can comprehend God. Those then who wish to know what God is, and to study Him, let them know that it is forbidden. They would become mad. All created light must fail here. What God is, passes the comprehension of every creature. But Holy Scripture, nature, and all the creatures show us that He is. We shall believe the articles of faith without trying to penetrate them, for that is impossible while we are here: this is sobriety. The difficult and subtle teachings of the inspired writings we shall only explain in accordance with the life of Christ and His saints. Man will study nature and the Scriptures, and every creature; and will seek to learn from them only what may be to his own advantage. This is sobriety of spirit.

A man will maintain sobriety of the senses, and he will subdue by reason his animal faculties, that the animal pleasure in food and drink may not delight him too much, but that he may eat and drink as a sick man takes a potion, because it is his duty to preserve his strength for the service of God. This is sobriety of body. A man will preserve moderation in words and actions, in silence and speech, in eating and drinking, in what he does and abstains from doing, as Holy Church enjoins and the saints give the example.

By moderation and sobriety of spirit within, a man maintains constancy and perseverance in the faith, that purity of intelligence and calmness of reason which are necessary to understand the truth, readiness to bend to the will of God with regard to every virtue, peace of heart and serenity of conscience. Thanks to this virtue, he possesses assured peace in God and in himself.

By moderation and sobriety in the use of the bodily faculties, he often preserves health and contentment of the bodily nature, his honour in external relations, and his good name. And thus he is at peace with himself and with his neighbour. For he attracts and rejoices all men of good will, by his moderation and sobriety. And he escapes the sixth deadly sin, which is want of temperance, and gluttony. It is of this that Christ said: "Blessed are the peacemakers, for they shall be called the children of God." For being like unto the Son, who has made peace in all creatures who desire it, and who make peace in their turn, by moderation and sobriety, the Son will divide among them the heritage of His Father, and they will possess this heritage with Him throughout eternity.

ON PURITY

FROM this sobriety are born purity of soul and body, for none can be absolutely pure in body and soul, save he who follows after sobriety in body and soul. Purity of spirit consists in this--that a man cleaves to no creature with any passionate desire, but attaches himself to God only; for one may use all the creatures while rejoicing in God only. Purity of spirit makes a man attach himself to God above intelligence and above the senses, and above all the gifts which God may bestow upon the soul; for all that the creature receives in its intelligence or in its senses purity desires to transcend, and to repose in God only. We should approach the sacrament of the altar not for the sake of the delights, the pleasure, the peace, or the sweetness which we find there, but for the glory of God only, and that we may grow in all the virtues. This is purity of spirit.

Purity of heart signifies that a man turns towards God without hesitation in every bodily temptation and every disturbance of nature, in the freedom of his will abandoning himself to Him with a new confidence and a firm resolve to abide always with God. For to consent to sin, or to the animal desires of the bodily nature, is a separation from God.

Purity of body means that a man abstains from impure actions of every kind, when his conscience assures him that they are impure and contrary to the commandments, to the glory, and to the will of God.

Thanks to these three kinds of purity, the seventh deadly sin, that of wantonness, is conquered and driven away. Wantonness is a voluptuous inclination of the spirit, leading away from God towards a created thing; it is the impure act of the flesh outside what Holy Church permits, and the carnal occupation of the heart in some taste or desire for a creature. I do not here refer to those sudden stirrings of love or desire which none can escape.

You now know that purity of spirit preserves men in the likeness of God, without care for the creatures, inclined towards God and united to Him. The chastity of the body is compared to the whiteness of the lily and to the purity of the angels. In its resistance to temptation, it is compared to the redness of the rose, and to the nobility of the martyrs. If it is preserved for love of God and in His honour, it is then perfect, and it is compared to the heliotrope, for it is one of the highest adornments of nature.

Purity of heart renews and increases the grace of God. In purity of heart all the virtues are inspired, practised, and preserved. It keeps and preserves the outer senses, it subdues and binds the animal desires within, and it is the ornament of all the inner life. It is the exclusion of the heart from things of earth and from all lies, and its inclusion among the things of heaven and all truth. And this is why Christ has said: "Blessed are the pure in heart, for they shall see God." This is the vision in which consists our eternal joy, and all our reward, and our entrance into bliss. This is why a man will be sober and moderate in everything, and will keep himself from every occasion which might tarnish the purity of his soul and body.

ON THE THREE ENEMIES WHO ARE TO BE CONQUERED BY JUSTICE

IF we wish to possess this virtue and to repulse these enemies, we must have justice, and we must practise it, and preserve it even until our death, in purity of heart, for we have three powerful enemies who try to attack us at all times, in all states, and in many different ways. If we make our peace with any one of them and follow him, we are vanquished, for they are in league with each other in all wickedness and injustice. These three enemies are the devil, the world, and our own flesh, which is the nearest to us, and is often the worst and most mischievous of our foes. For our animal desires are the weapons with which our enemies fight against us. Idleness, and indifference to virtue and the glory of God are the cause and occasion of war and combat. But the weakness of our natures, our negligence and ignorance of truth are the sword by which our enemies wound us and sometimes conquer us.

And this is why we must be divided in ourselves. The lower part of ourselves, which is animal and contrary to the virtues, we ought to hate and persecute and cause it to suffer by means of penitence and austerities, so that it may be always crushed down and submissive to reason, and that justice, with purity of heart, may always keep the upper hand in all virtuous actions. And all the pains, sorrows, and persecutions which God makes us suffer at the hands of those who are enemies to virtue, we shall endure with joy, in honour of God and for the glory of virtue, and in the hope of obtaining and possessing justice in purity of heart; for Christ said: "Blessed are those who are persecuted for righteousness' sake, for theirs is the kingdom of heaven." For righteousness preserved in virtue and in virtuous actions is a coin of the same weight and value as the kingdom of heaven, and it is by it that we may purchase and obtain eternal life. By these virtues a man goes forth towards God and towards himself, in good conduct, virtue, and justice.

ON THE KINGDOM OF THE SOUL

HE who wishes to obtain and preserve these virtues, will adorn, occupy, and order his soul like a kingdom. Free will is the king of the soul. It is free by nature, and more free still by grace. It will be crowned with a crown or diadem named Charity. We shall receive this crown and this kingdom from the Emperor, who is the Lord, the sovereign and king of kings, and we shall possess, rule, and preserve this kingdom in His name. This king, free will, will dwell in the highest town in the kingdom--that is to say, in the concupiscent faculty of the soul. He will be adorned and clad with a robe in two parts. The right side of his robe will be a virtue called strength, that he may be strong and powerful to overcome all obstacles and sojourn in the heaven, in the palace of the supreme Emperor, and to bend with love and ardent self-surrender his crowned head before the supreme monarch. This is the proper work of charity. By it we receive the crown, by it we adorn the crown, and by it we keep and possess the kingdom throughout eternity. The left side of the robe will be a cardinal virtue, called moral courage. Thanks to it, free will, the king, will subdue all immorality, will accomplish all virtue, and will have the power to keep his kingdom even until death. The king will choose councillors in his country, the wisest in the land. They will be two divine virtues, knowledge and discretion, illuminated by divine grace. They will dwell near the king, in a palace called the reasonable force of the soul. They will be crowned and adorned with a moral virtue called temperance, that the king may always act and refrain from acting according to their advice. By knowledge we shall purge our conscience from all its faults and adorn it with all virtues; and, thanks to discretion, we shall give and take, do and not do, speak and be silent, fast and eat, listen and answer, and act in all ways according to knowledge and discretion clad in their moral virtue, which is called temperance or moderation.

This king, free will, will also establish in his kingdom a judge, who will be justice, which is a divine virtue when it is born from love. And it is one of the highest moral virtues. This judge will dwell in the conscience, in the middle of the kingdom in the irascible faculty. And he will be adorned with a moral virtue called prudence. For justice without prudence cannot be perfect. This judge, justice, will traverse the kingdom with royal powers, accompanied by wise counsel and his own prudence. He will promote and dismiss, he will judge and condemn, will condemn to death and acquit, will mutilate, blind, and restore to sight, will exalt and abase and organise, will punish and chastise according to justice, and will destroy all vices. The people of the kingdom-- that is to say, all the faculties of the soul, will be supported by humility and the fear of God, submitting to Him in all the virtues, each after its own manner. He who has thus occupied, preserved, and ordered the kingdom of his soul, has gone forth, by love and the virtues, towards God, towards himself, and towards his neighbour. This is the third of the four principal points which Christ speaks of when He says, Go forth.

ON THE THREEFOLD MEETING OF THE SOUL

WHEN a man has, by the grace of God, eyes to see, and a pure conscience, and when he has considered the three comings of Christ, our Bridegroom, and lastly when he has gone forth by the virtues, then takes place the meeting with our Bridegroom, and this is the fourth and last point. In this meeting consist all our blessedness, and the beginning and the end of all the virtues, and without this meeting no virtue can be practised.

He who wishes to meet Christ as his well-beloved Bridegroom, and to possess in Him and with Him eternal life, must meet Christ, now in time, in three points or in three manners. First, he must love God in everything wherein we shall merit eternal life. Secondly, he must attach himself to nothing which he might love as much as or more than God. Thirdly, he must repose in God with all his might, above all creatures and above all the gifts of God, and above all acts of virtue and above all the sensible graces which God might spread abroad in his soul and body.

Now understand: he who has God for his end must have Him present to himself, by some divine reason. That is to say, he must have in view Him who is the Lord of heaven, and of earth, and of every creature, Him who died for him, and who can and will give him eternal salvation. In whatever mode and under whatever name he represents God, as Lord of every creature, it is well. If he takes some divine Person, and in Him sees the essence and power of the divine nature, it is well. If he regards God as saviour, redeemer, creator, governor, as blessedness, power, wisdom, truth, goodness, it is well. Though the names which we ascribe to God are numerous, the sublime nature of God is simple and unnameable by the creatures. But we give Him all these names by reason of His nobleness and incomprehensible sublimity, and because we cannot name or proclaim Him completely. See now under what mode and by what knowledge God will be present to our intention. For to have God for our aim is to see spiritually. To this quest belong also affection and love, for to know God and be without love aids and advances us not a whit, and has no savour. This is why a man, in all his actions, must bend lovingly towards God, whom he seeks and loves above everything. This, then, is the meeting with God by means of intention and love.

In order that the sinner may turn from his sins in a meritorious penitence, he must meet God by contrition, free conversion, and a sincere intention to serve God for ever, and to sin no more. Then, at this meeting, he receives from the mercy of God the assured hope of eternal salvation and the pardon of his sins, and he receives the foundation of all the virtues, faith, hope, and charity, and the good will to practise all the virtues. If this man advances in the light of faith, and observes all the works of Christ, all His sufferings and all His promises, and all that He has done for us and will do to the day of judgment and through eternity; if he examines all this for his soul's health, he must needs meet with Christ; and Christ must needs be present to his soul, so grateful and full of thankfulness. So his faith is fortified, and he is impelled more inwardly and powerfully towards all the virtues. If he still progresses in the works of virtue, he must again meet with Christ, by the annihilation of self. Let him not seek his own things; let him set before him no extraneous ends; let him be discreet in his actions; let him set God always before him, and the praise and glory of God; and let him so continue till his death; then his reason will be enlightened and his charity increased, and he will become more pious and apt for all the virtues. We shall set God before us in every good work; in bad works we cannot set Him before us. We shall not have two intentions--that is to say, we shall not seek God at the same time as something else, but all our intention must be subordinated to God and not contrary to Him, but of one and the same kind, so that it may help us and give us an impulse which may lead us more easily to God. Then and then only is a man in the right road. Moreover, we shall rest rather upon Him who is our aim and our goal and the object of our love, than upon the messengers whom He sends us--that is to say, His gifts. The soul will rest constantly upon God, above all the adornments and presents which His messengers may bring. The messengers sent by the soul are intention, love, and desire. They carry to God all our good works and virtues. Above all these, the soul will rest on God, its Beloved, above all multiplicity. This is the manner in which we shall meet Christ all through our life, in all our actions and virtues, by right intention, that we may meet Him at the hour of our death in the light of glory.

This mode, as you have learnt, is called the active life. It is necessary to all men; or at least they must not live in a manner contrary to any virtue, though they may not attain the degree of perfection in all the virtues which I have described. For to live contrary to the virtues is to live in sin, as Christ has said: "He that is not with me is against me." He who is not humble is proud, and he who is proud belongs not to God. We must always possess a virtue and be in a state of grace, or possess what is contrary to that virtue and be in a state of sin. May every man examine and prove himself, and order his life as I have here described.

ON THE DESIRE TO KNOW GOD AS HE IS, IN THE NATURE OF HIS GODHEAD

THE man who thus lives, in this perfection, as I have here described it, and who devotes all his life and actions to the honour and glory of God, and who seeks and loves God above all things, is often seized by the desire to see and know Christ, this Bridegroom who was made man for love of him, who laboured in love even till death, who drove away from him sin and the enemy, who gave him His grace, who gave him Himself, who left him His sacraments and promised him His kingdom. When a man considers all this, he is exceedingly desirous to see Christ his Bridegroom, and to know what He is in Himself While He only knows Him in His works he is not satisfied. So he will do like Zacchaeus, the publican, who desired to see Jesus Christ. He will go in front of the crowd--that is to say, the multitude of the creatures, for they make us so little and short, that we cannot perceive God. And he will climb the tree of faith, which grows from above downwards, for its roots are in the Godhead. This tree has twelve branches, which are the twelve articles of faith. The lower branches speak of the humanity of Christ, and of the things which concern the salvation of our body and soul. The higher part of the tree speaks of the Godhead, of the Trinity of the Divine Persons and the Unity of the Divine Nature. A man will strive to reach the unity at the top of the tree, for it is there that Jesus must pass with all His gifts. Here Jesus comes, and sees the man, and tells Him in the light of faith that He is, according to His Godhead, immeasurable and incomprehensible, inaccessible and abysmal, and that He surpasses all created light and all finite comprehension. This is the highest knowledge acquired in the active life, to recognise thus, in the light of faith, that God is inconceivable and unknowable. In this light Christ saith to the desire of a man: "Come down quickly, for I must lodge at thy house to-day." This rapid descent to which God invites him is nothing else but a descent, by desire and love, into the abyss of the Godhead, to which no intelligence can attain in crested light. But where intelligence remains outside, love and desire enter. The soul thus bending towards God, by the intention of love, above all that the intellect can comprehend, rests and abides in God, and God abides in her. Then mounting by desire, above the multitude of the creatures, above the work of the senses, above the light of nature, she meets Christ in the light of faith, and is enlightened, and recognises that God is unknowable and inconceivable. Finally, bending by her desires towards this inconceivable God, she meets Christ and is loaded with His gifts; by living and resting upon Him, above all His gifts, above herself and above all the creatures, she dwells in God and God in her.

This is how you will meet Christ at the summit of the active life, if you have as your foundations justice, charity, and humility; and if you have built a house above--that is to say, the virtues here described, and if you have met Christ by faith--that is to say, by faith and the intention of love, you dwell in God and God dwells in you, and you possess the active life.

This is the first explanation of the word of Jesus Christ our Bridegroom, when He said, "See, the Bridegroom cometh; go forth to meet Him."

BOOK II

THE SUBJECTS OF THE SECOND BOOK

THE prudent virgin--that is to say, the pure soul, who has renounced the things of earth, and lives henceforth for God in virtue, has taken in the vessel of her heart the oil of charity and of divine works by means of the lamp of an unstained conscience. But when Christ, her Bridegroom, withdraws His consolations and the fresh outpouring of His gifts, the soul becomes heavy and torpid.

At midnight--that is to say, when it is least expected, a spiritual cry resounds in the soul: "See, the Bridegroom cometh, go forth to meet Him." We shall now speak of this seeing, and of the inward coming of Christ, and of the spiritual going forth of the man to meet Jesus, and we shall explain these four conditions of an inward life, exalted and full of desire, to which all men attain not, but many reach it by means of the virtues and their inward courage.

In these words, Christ teaches us four things. In the first, He requires that our intelligence shall be enlightened with a supernatural light. This is what we observe in the word, "See." In the next words He shows us what we ought to see--that is to say, the inward coming of our Bridegroom of eternal truth. This is His meaning when He says: "The Bridegroom cometh." In the third place, in the words "go forth," He bids us go forth in inward actions according to righteousness. In the fourth place, He shows us the end and motive of all our works, the meeting with our Bridegroom Jesus Christ in the joyous unity of His adorable Godhead.

HOW WE MAY GAIN SUPERNATURAL VISION BY INTERNAL EXERCISES

NOW let us speak of the first word. Christ saith, "See." Three things are required by him who would see supernaturally in interior exercises. The first is the light of the divine grace, but in a far more sublime manner than can be felt in the external, active life. The second is a stripping off of extraneous images and a denudation of the heart, so that a man may be free from images, and attachments to every creature. The third is a free conversion of the will, by means of a concentration of all the bodily and spiritual faculties, and complete deliverance from all inordinate affections. Thus this will flows together into the unity of the Godhead and of our own mind, so that the reasonable creature may be able to obtain and possess supernaturally the sublime unity of God. It is for this that God made the heaven and earth and mankind, it is for this that He was made man, and taught us by word and example by what way we should come to this unity. And then in the ardour of His love He endured to die, and He ascended to heaven, and opened to us this unity in which we may possess felicity and eternal blessedness.

ON THE THREEFOLD NATURAL UNITY OF MAN

NOW consider attentively: there are three kinds of natural unity in all men, and, moreover, of supernatural unity among the just. The first and supreme unity of man is in God; for all creatures are immanent in this unity, and if they were to be separated from God, they would be annihilated, and would become nothing. This unity is essential in us according to nature, whether we are good or bad. And without our co-operation it makes us neither holy nor blessed. This unity we possess in ourselves, and nevertheless above us, as a beginning and support of our life and essence.

Another unity exists in us naturally--that of the supreme forces, in so far as they actively take their natural origin in the unity of the spirit or of the thoughts. This is the same unity as that which is immanent in God, but it is taken here actively and there essentially. Nevertheless the spirit is entirely in each unity according to the integrity of its substance. We possess this unity in ourselves, above the sensitive part of us; and thence are born memory, intelligence, and will, and all the power of spiritual works. In this unity the soul is called spirit.

The third unity which is in us naturally is the foundation of bodily forces in the unity of the heart, the source and origin of bodily life. The soul possesses this unity in the lively centre of the heart, and from it flow all the material works and the five senses, and the soul draws from thence its name of soul (anima); for it is the source of life, and animates the body--that is to say, it makes it living and preserves it in life. These three unities are in man naturally, as a life and a kingdom. In the inferior unity we are sensible and animal, in the intermediate unity we are rational and spiritual; and in the superior unity we are preserved according to our essence. And this exists in all men, naturally.

Now these three unities are adorned and cultivated naturally, like a kingdom and an eternal abode, by the virtues, in charity and in the active life. And they are adorned still better and more gloriously cultivated by the internal exercises of a spiritual life. But most gloriously and blessedly of all by a supernatural contemplative life.

The inferior unity, which is corporeal, is adorned and cultivated supernaturally by external practices, by perfect conduct, by the example of Christ and the saints, by carrying the cross with Christ, by submitting our nature to the command of Holy Church and the teachings of the saints, according to the forces of nature and prudence.

The other unity which resides in the spirit and which is absolutely spiritual, is adorned and cultivated supernaturally by the three Divine gifts, Faith, Hope, and Charity, and by the influx of grace and Divine gifts, and by good will directed to all the virtues, and the desire to follow the example of Christ and of holy Christendom.

The third and supreme unity is above our intelligence and yet essentially in us. We cultivate it supernaturally when in all our works of virtue we have in view only the glory of God, without any other desire but to repose in Him, above thought, above ourselves, and above everything. And this is the unity from which we flowed out when we were created, and where we abide according to our essence, and towards which we endeavour to return by love. These are the virtues which adorn this triple unity in the active life.

Now we proceed to say how this triple unity is adorned more sublimely and cultivated more nobly by interior exercises joined to the active life. When a man, by love and right intention, elevates himself in all his works and in all his life towards the honour and glory of God, and seeks rest in God above all things, he will wait in humility and patience and abandonment of self and in the hope of new riches and new gifts, and he will not be troubled or anxious whether it pleases God to grant His gifts or to refuse them. So men prepare themselves for receiving an internal life of desires; even as a vessel is fitted and prepared, into which a precious liquid is to be poured. There is no vessel more noble than the loving soul, and no drink more necessary than the grace of God. Man will thus offer to God all his works and all his life, in a simple and right intention, and in a zest above his intention, above himself, and above everything, in the sublime unity in which God and the loving spirit are united without intermediary.

ON THE FIRST MODE OR DEGREE OF THE FIRST SPIRITUAL COMING OF CHRIST

THE first coming of Christ to those who are engaged in the exercises of desire is an internal and sensible current from the Holy Spirit, which impels and attracts us to all the virtues. We shall compare this coming to the splendour and power of the sun, which, so soon as it is risen, enlightens and warms the whole world in the twinkling of an eye. In the same way Christ, the eternal sun, burns and shines, dwelling at the highest point of the spirit, and enlightens and fires the lower part of man--that is to say, his physical heart and sense-faculties, and this is accomplished in less time than the twinkling of an eye, for the work of God is prompt; but the man in whom it takes place ought to be internally seeing by means of his spiritual eyes.

The sun burns in the East, in the middle of the world, on the mountains; there it hastens in the summer, and creates good fruits and strong wines, filling the earth with joy. The same sun shines in the West, at the end of the world; the country there is colder and the force of the heat less; nevertheless, it there produces a great number of good fruits, but not much wine. The men who dwell in the West part of themselves, abide in their external senses, and by their good intentions, their virtues, and their outer practices, by the grace of God produce abundant harvests of virtues of divers kinds, but they but rarely taste the wine of inward joy and spiritual consolation.

The man who wishes to experience the rays of the eternal sun, which is Christ Himself, will be seeing; and will dwell on the mountains of the East, by concentrating all his faculties, and lifting up his heart to God, free, and indifferent to joy and pain and all the creatures. There shines Christ, the sun of righteousness, on the free and exalted heart, and this is what I mean by the mountains. Christ, the glorious sun and divine effulgence, shines through and fires by his internal coming, and by the power of His Spirit, the free heart and all the powers of the soul. This is the first work of the internal coming in the exercises of desire. Just as fire inflames things which are thrown into it, so Christ inflames the hearts offered to Him in freedom and exultation at His internal coming, and He says in this coming: "Go forth by the exercises appropriate to this life."

ON UNITY OF HEART

FROM this heat is born unity of heart, for we cannot obtain true unity, unless the Spirit of God lights His flame in our heart. For this fire makes one and like unto itself all that it can overtop and transform. Unity gives a man the feeling of being concentrated with all his faculties on one point. It gives internal peace and repose of heart. Unity of heart is a bond which draws and binds together the body and the soul, and all exterior and interior forces, in the unity of love.

HOW THE VIRTUES PROCEED FROM UNITY

FROM this unity of heart is born inwardness or the internal life, for none can have inwardness unless he is one and united in himself; fervour or inwardness is the introversion of a man into his own heart, to comprehend and experience the internal operation or speech of God. Inwardness is a sensible flame of love, which the Spirit of God lights and kindles in a man, and a man knows not whence it comes, nor what has happened to him.

ON SENSIBLE LOVE

FROM inwardness is born a sensible love which penetrates the heart of man and the highest faculties of the soul. This love and delight none can experience who has not inwardness. Sensible love is the desire and appetite for God as for an eternal good in which all is contained. Sensible love renounces all the creatures, not as needs but as pleasures. Interior love feels itself touched from above by the eternal love which it must practise eternally Interior love willingly renounces and despises everything, in order to obtain that which it loves.

ON DEVOTION

FROM this sensible love is born devotion to God and His glory. For none can have a hungry devotion in his heart, unless he possesses the sensible love of God. Devotion excites and stimulates a man internally and externally to the service of God. It makes the body and soul abound in glory and merit in the eyes of God and men. God exacts devotion in all that we do. It purges the body and soul from all that might hold us back; it shows us the true path to blessedness.

ON GRATITUDE

FROM fervent devotion is born gratitude, for none can thank or praise God perfectly if he is not fervent and pious. We should thank God for everything here below, that we may be able to thank Him eternally above. Those who praise not God here, will be mute eternally. To praise God is the most joyous and delicious employment of the loving heart. There is no limit to the praises of God, for therein is our salvation, and we shall praise Him eternally.

Now hear a comparison, by which you may understand the exercise of gratitude. When the summer approaches and the sun mounts, it attracts the moisture of the earth along the stems and branches of the trees, whence come green leaves, flowers, and fruit. Even so when Christ, the eternal sun, rises in our hearts, He sends His light and heat upon our desires, and draws the heart away from all the manifold things of earth, creating unity and inwardness, and makes the heart grow and become green by interior love, and makes loving devotion flourish, and makes us bear the fruits of gratitude and love, and preserves these fruits eternally in the humble pain of our inability to praise and serve Him enough.

Here ends the first of the four chief kinds ot interior exercises, which adorn the lower part of a man.

HOW TO INCREASE INWARDNESS BY HUMILITY

BUT in thus comparing to the splendour and power of the sun the modes in which Jesus Christ comes, we shall find in the sun another virtue or influence which makes the fruit more early ripe and more abundant.

When the sun rises to a very great height, and enters the sign of the Twins-- that is to say, into a double thing, but of the same nature, in the middle of the month of May, the sun has a double power over the flowers, herbs, and all that grows upon the earth. If at that time the planets which rule nature are well ordered according to the season of the year, the sun shines brightly on the earth, and attracts the moisture in the atmosphere. Hence are born dew and rain, and the fruits of the ground increase and multiply.

Even so when Christ, that bright sun, rises in our heart above all other things, and when the requirements of material nature, which are contrary to the spirit, are well regulated according to reason, when we possess the virtues as I have said above, and when, lastly, we offer and restore to God, by the ardour of charity, and with gratitude and love, the delight and peace which we find in the virtues, from all these are born, at times, a gentle rain of new internal consolations, and a celestial dew of divine sweetness. This dew and rain make all the virtues increase and multiply day by day, if we put no hindrance in their way. This is a new and special operation, and a new coming of Christ into the loving heart.

ON PURE SATISFACTION OF THE HEART

FROM this sweetness is born satisfaction of heart, and of all the bodily faculties, so that a man imagines that he is inwardly embraced in the divine bands of love. This pleasure and consolation is greater and more delicious to body and soul than all the pleasures granted on earth, even if a man could enjoy them to the full. In this pleasure God sinks into the heart by means of His gifts with such a profusion of delights, consolations, and joys, that the heart overflows internally.

ON THE OBSTACLES WHICH WE ENCOUNTER IN THIS STATE

THIS coming, or kind of coming, is granted to beginners, when they turn from the world, when their conversion is complete, and they abandon all the consolations of earth to live for God only; nevertheless they are still weak, and need milk and not strong meat, such as great temptations and the hiding of God's face. At this season frost and fog often injure them, for they are in the middle of the May of the interior life. The frost is to wish to be something, or to imagine that we are something, or to be somewhat attached to ourselves, or to believe that we have deserved consolations and are worthy of them. The fog is the wish to rest upon internal consolations and pains. This obscures the atmosphere of reason, and the ilowers, which were about to unfold and bloom and bear fruits, shut up again. This is why we lose the knowledge of truth, and nevertheless we sometimes keep certain false sweetnesses granted by the enemy, which at the last lead men astray.

HOW ONE OUGHT TO BEHAVE IN THIS CASE

I WISH to give you here a brief comparison, that you may not go astray, and that you may be able to behave wisely in this case. Observe the wise bee, and imitate her. She dwells in unity, in the midst of the assembly of her kind, and she goes forth, not during a storm, but when the weather is calm and bright, and the sun shines; and she flies towards every flower where she may find sweetness. She rests not on any flower, neither for its beauty nor for its sweetness, but draws out from the cups of the flowers their sweetness and clearness--that is to say, the honey and wax, and she brings them back to the unity which is formed of the assembly of all the bees, that the honey and wax may be put to good use.

The expanded heart on which Christ, the eternal sun, shines, grows and blooms under His rays, and from it flow all the interior forces in joy and sweetness.

Now the wise man will act like the bee, and will try to settle, with affection, intelligence, and prudence, on all the gifts and all the sweetness that he has experienced, and on all the good that God has done to him. He will not rest on any flower of the gifts, but laden with gratitude and praise he will fly back towards the unity where he wishes to dwell, and to rest with God eternally.

ON THE THIRD MODE OF THE SPIRITUAL COMING OF CHRIST

WHEN the sun in heaven reaches its highest point, in the sign of the Crab-- that is to say, when it can go no higher, but must begin to go backwards, then the greatest heat of the year begins. The sun attracts the moisture, the earth dries, and the fruits ripen. In the same way, when Christ, the divine sun, arises above the highest summit of our heart--that is to say, above all His gifts, consolations and sweetnesses, and if we do not rest in any of these, however sweet, but return always with humble praises to the source from which these gifts flow, Christ stops and remains lifted up above the summit of our heart, and desires to attract all our powers to Himself.

This invitation is an irradiation of Christ, the eternal sun, and causes in the heart a joy and pleasure so great that the heart cannot close again after such an expansion, without pain. A man is wounded internally and feels the smart of love. To be wounded by love is the sweetest sensation and the most grievous pain that can be experienced. To be wounded by love is a sure sign that we shall be cured. This spiritual wound does us good and harm at the same time.

ON THE FOURTH KIND OF THE SPIRITUAL COMING OF CHRIST

NOW I wish to speak of the fourth kind of coming of Jesus Christ, which exalts and perfects the man in his interior exercises, according to the lower part of his being. But having compared all the interior comings to the shining of the sun, we will continue to speak, while following the course of the seasons, of the other effects and works of the sun.

When the sun begins to descend the sky, it enters the sign of the Virgin, so called because this period of the year becomes barren like a virgin. The glorious virgin Mary, mother of Christ, full of joys and rich in all the virtues, ascended to heaven at this season. The heat begins then to diminish, and men gather, for use during the whole year, the ripe fruits which can be used long after, such as corn and the grape. And they sow part of the corn, that it may be multiplied for the use of men. At this season all the solar work of the year is finished. In the same way, when Christ, the glorious sun, has risen to the zenith in the heart of men, and begins to descend, so as to hide the splendour of His divine beams and to leave a man alone, the heat and impatience of love diminish. Now this occultation of Christ and the withdrawal of His light and heat are the first work and the new coming of this mode. Now Christ says spiritually in a man: "Go forth in the manner that I now show thee"; and the man goes forth, and finds himself poor, miserable, and desolate. Here all the storm, all the passion and eagerness of love grow cold; summer becomes autumn, and all his wealth is changed into great poverty. And the man begins to complain by reason of his misery; what is become of his ardent love, his inwardness, his gratitude, the interior consolations, the heartfelt joys? Where has it all gone? How comes it that all is dead within him? He is like a scholar who has lost his knowledge and his work; and nature is often troubled by such losses. Sometimes these unhappy ones are deprived of the good things of earth, of their friends and relations, and are deserted by all the creatures; their holiness is mistrusted and despised, men put a bad construction upon all the works of their life, and they are rejected and disdained by all those who surround them; and sometimes they are afflicted with diverse diseases; and some of them fall into bodily temptations, or into spiritual temptations, the most dangerous of all. From this misery are born the fear of falling, and a sort of half-doubt, and this is the extreme point where we can stop without despair. Let such men seek out the good, complain to them, show them their distress, and ask their help, and implore the aid of Holy Church, and of all just men.

WHAT A MAN OUGHT TO DO WHEN HE IS ABANDONED

A MAN will here observe humbly that he has nothing but his distress, and he will say in his resignation and self-abnegation the words of holy Job: "The Lord gave, and the Lord hath taken away; He hath done what seemed good to Him; blessed be the name of the Lord." And he will leave himself in everything, and will say and think in his heart: "Lord, I am as willing to be poor, lacking all that Thou hast taken from me, as I should be to be rich, if such were Thy will, and if it were for Thine honour. It is not my will according to nature which must be accomplished, but Thy will, and my will according to my spirit, O Lord; for I belong to Thee, and I should love as well to be Thine in hell as in heaven, if that could serve Thy glory; and therefore, O Lord, accomplish in me the excellence of Thy will." From all these pains and acts of resignation, a man will derive an inward joy, and he will offer himself into the hands of God, and will rejoice to be able to suffer in His honour. And if he so perseveres, he will taste inward pleasures such as he has never had before; for nothing so rejoices the lover of God as to feel that he is His beloved. And if he is truly exalted as far as this mode, in the path of virtue, it is not necessary for him to have passed through all the states which we have described above; for he feels within himself in action, in humble obedience, in patience, and in resignation, the source of all the virtues. It is thus that this mode is eternally sure.

At this season the sun in the sky enters the sign of the Scales, for the day and night are equal, and the sun balances the light and the darkness. In the same way Jesus Christ is in the sign of the Scales for the resigned man; and whether He grants sweetness or bitterness, darkness or light, whatever He chooses to send him, the man keeps his balance, all things are equal to him except sin, which has been driven away once for all. When every consolation has been thus withdrawn from these resigned men, when they believe that they have lost all their virtues and that they are abandoned by God and all the creatures, if they then know how to reap the divers fruits, their corn and wine are ready and ripe. That is to say, that all that the bodily virtues can suffer will be offered by them to God with joy, without resistance to His supreme will. All the exterior and interior virtues, which they formerly practised with joy in the light of love, they will now practise courageously and laboriously, and will offer them to God, and never will they have so much merit in His eyes. Never will they have been more noble or more beautiful. All the consolations which God formerly granted, they will allow to be stripped from them with joy, since it is for the glory of God. It is thus that the virtues become perfect, and that sadness is transformed into an eternal vintage. These men--their life and their patience--improve and teach all who know and live near them, and thus it is that the wheat of their virtues is sown and multiplied for the good of all just men.

This is the fourth kind of coming which, according to the bodily faculties and the lower part of his being, adorns and perfects a man in interior exercises.

HOW THESE FOUR MODES ARE FOUND IN JESUS CHRIST

WE must needs walk in the light if we wish not to lose our way, and we must observe Jesus Christ, who has taught us these four modes, and has preceded us in them. Christ, the bright sun, rises in the heaven of the sublime Trinity and in the dawn of His glorious mother the virgin Mary, who was and is the dawn of all the graces. Now observe. Christ had and still has the first mode, for He was unique and united. In Him were and are collected and united all the virtues which have ever been practised, and which ever will be, and besides this, all the creatures who will cultivate these virtues. He was thus in an unique sense the Son of the Father, and united to human nature. And He was equally full of inwardness, for it was He who brought upon earth the fire which has consumed all the saints and all good men. And He had a sensible and faithful love for His Father, and for all who will have joy in Him eternally, and His pitiful and loving heart sighed and glowed with love for all men, before His Father. All His life and all His actions, within and without, and all His words, were praises of His Father. This is the first mode.

Christ, the sun of love, blazed and shone yet more brightly and warmly, for in Him was and is the fullness of all gifts. This is why the heart of Christ, and His character, and His habits and His service, overflowed with pity, sweetness, humility, and generosity. So gracious was He and so loving, that His manners and His personality attracted all whose nature was good. He was the pure lily in the midst of the flowers of the field, from which the good were to draw the honey of eternal sweetness and eternal consolations. According to His humanity He thanked His eternal Father for all the gifts which were ever granted to humanity, and praised Him, for His Father is the Father of all gifts, and He rested on Him, according to the highest faculties of His soul, above all gifts, in the sublime unity of God from which all the gifts flow; thus He had the second mode.

Christ, the glorious sun, blazed and shone yet higher, and more brightly and warmly; for during all His days on earth, all His bodily faculties were invited and pressed to the sublime glory and bliss which He now experiences in His senses and body. And He was inclined thereto Himself, according to His desires; and nevertheless He willed to remain in this exile, till the time which the Father had foreseen and fixed from all eternity. Thus He had the third mode. When the time came at which Christ was to reap and carry away to the eternal kingdom the fruits of all the virtues which ever have been and ever will be practised, the eternal sun began to descend; for Christ humbled Himself, and gave up His bodily life into the hands of His enemies. And he was misunderstood and deserted by His friends in so great a distress; and all consolation, within and without, was withdrawn from His nature; and it was overwhelmed with misery, pain, and contempt, and paid all the debt which our sins justly incurred. All this He suffered in humble patience, and He accomplished the greatest works of love in this resignation, whereby He received and purchased our eternal inheritance. It is thus that the lower part of His noble humanity was adorned, for it was in it that He suffered this pain for our sins. It is on this account that He is called the Saviour of the world, and that He is glorified and raised up and seated on the right hand of His Father, and that He reigns in power. And every creature, on the earth, above the earth, and under the earth, bends the knee for ever before His glorious name.

HOW A MAN SHOULD LIVE IF HE DESIRES TO BE ENLIGHTENED

THE man who, in true obedience to the commandments of God, lives in the moral virtues, and moreover exercises himself in the interior virtues, after the direction and impulse of the Holy Spirit, acting and speaking according to righteousness, and who seeks not his own interests in time or in eternity, and who supports with true patience obscurity and affliction and every kind of misery, and who thanks God for everything, and offers himself in humble resignation, has received the first coming of Jesus Christ according to interior exercises. When this man is purified and pacified, and turns back upon himself according to his lower nature, he may be internally enlightened, if he asks it, and if God judges that the right time has come. It may also happen that he is enlightened from the beginning of his conversion, so that he may offer himself entirely to the will of God and give up all possession of himself, which is the supreme end. But if he is to follow any further the road which I have shown, in the exterior and at the same time in the interior life, it will be much easier for him than for the man who has been raised straight from the bottom, for the former will have more light than the latter.

ON ANOTHER COMING OF CHRIST

NOW we are about to speak of another mode of the coming of Christ, in interior exercises, which adorn, enlighten, and enrich a man, according to the three supreme faculties of his soul. We shall compare this coming to a life-giving fountain from which flow three rivers.

This fountain is the fullness of divine grace in the unity of our spirit. There resides grace essentially in its permanence, like a full fountain, and it flows out actively by its rivers into each of the faculties of the soul, according to their needs. These rivers are a special influx, or operation of God in the highest faculties, in which God operates in various manners by the intermediary of His grace.

HOW THE FIRST RIVER FLOWS INTO THE MEMORY

THE first river of grace, which God causes to flow in this coming, is a pure simplicity which shines without distinction in the spirit. This river takes its source in the fountain, in the unity of the spirit, and flows directly downwards, and penetrates all the faculties of the soul, both higher and lower, and lifts them up out of all multiplicity and all over-occupation, and makes a simplicity in a man, and gives and shows him an internal bond in the unity of his spirit. A man is thus lifted up according to his memory, and delivered from strange and irrelevant thoughts, and from inconstancy. Now Christ in this light demands a going forth, according to the mode of this light and this coming. Then the man goes forth, and observes himself that by virtue of the simple light that is spread abroad in him he is united, established, penetrated and fixed in the unity of his spirit or of his thoughts. Here the man is exalted and established in a new essence; he turns his thoughts inwards, and rests his memory on the naked truth, above all sensuous images and above all multiplicity. There the man possesses essentially and supernaturally the unity of his spirit, for his own dwelling, and as an heritage of his own for ever. He always has an inclination towards that same unity, and this unity will have an eternal and loving inclination towards the more sublime unity where the Father and the Son are united with all the saints in the bands of the Holy Spirit.

HOW THE SECOND RIVER ENLIGHTENS THE INTELLIGENCE

THROUGH internal love, and loving inclination towards union with God, is born the second river from the fullness of grace, in unity of spirit, and this is a spiritual brightness which flows and sheds light through the intelligence, but with distinctions in the diverse modes. For this light shows and gives to the spirit, in the truth, the discretion in all the virtues. But this light is not placed altogether in our power, for though we have it always in our soul, God makes it speak or keep silence, and He can manifest or hide it, give or withdraw it, at all times and under all conditions, for this light is His. Such men do not absolutely need revelations, nor to be drawn up above sense, for their life and abode and habits and essence are in the spirit above sense and sensibility. And God shows them what He wills and what is necessary for them. Nevertheless God, if He wished, could withdraw their exterior sense, and show them, from within, unknown symbols and future things, in diverse manners.

Now Christ desires that this man should go forth, and go into the light, according to the mode of this light. This enlightened man will therefore go forth and observe his state and his life within and without, in order to know if he is perfectly like Christ according to His humanity and also according to His divinity. And this man will lift up his eyes, enlightened by enlightened reason, in intelligible truth, and will observe and consider, as a creature can, the sublime nature of God, and the unlimited attributes which are in God.

It is then necessary to consider and examine the sublime nature of God; how it contains simplicity and purity, inaccessible height and abysmal depth, incomprehensible extension and eternal duration; dark silence and wild waste; repose of all the saints in unity and joy in itself and in all the saints in eternity. This enlightened man will also examine the attributes of the Father in the

Godhead, how He is all-powerful, the creator, mover, preserver, beginning and end, cause and existence of all creatures; this is what the bright river of grace shows to the enlightened reason. It shows also the attributes of the eternal Word, abysmal wisdom and truth, model of every creature and of all life, eternal norm of things, unveiled contemplation and intuition into everything, brightness and illumination of all saints, according to their merits, in heaven and on earth. But this bright river shows also to the enlightened reason the attributes of the Holy Spirit; inconceivable charity and generosity, pity and mercy, infinite watchfulness and faithfulness, immense and inconceivable riches flowing with delights through all heavenly spirits, ardent flame consuming all in unity, effluent fountain, preparation of all the saints for their eternal blessedness, and their introduction thereto; enveloping and penetrating the Father, the Son, and all the saints in joyous unity.

ON THE STATE OF AMAZEMENT AT THE DIVINE EFFLUENCE

THE incomprehensible wealth and sublimity, and the universal generosity which flow from the divine nature, bring a man into a state of amazement; and above all he admires the communication of God and His effluence above everything, for he sees the inconceivable essence, which is the common joy of God and all the saints. And he sees that the three divine Persons are a common effluence in works, in graces, and in glory, in nature and above nature, in all conditions and in all times, in the saints and in men, in heaven and on earth, in all reasonable and irrational creatures, according to each one's merits, needs, and powers of receiving. God is common to all, with all His gifts, the angels are common, the soul is common in all its faculties, in all life, in all the members, and all in each, for one cannot divide it, except by reason. For the higher and lower faculties, the spirit and the soul, are distinct according to reason, but one in nature. Thus God is entirely and specially present to each one, and nevertheless common to all the creatures, for by Him are all things, and on Him depend the heaven, the earth, and the whole of nature. When a man thus observes the astonishing wealth and sublimity of the divine nature, and all the manifold gifts which He grants and offers to His creatures, he is lifted up internally by wonder at such manifold riches and sublimity; and from thence arises a singular inward joy of spirit, and a vast confidence in God; and this internal joy surrounds and penetrates all the faculties of the soul in inwardness of spirit.

HOW THE THIRD RIVER CONFIRMS THE WILL

FROM this joy and fullness of graces, and divine faithfulness, there is born and flows out the third river in this same unity of spirit. This river, like a flame, lights up the spirit and absorbs all things in unity. And it causes to overflow and flood with rich gifts and singular nobility, all the faculties of the soul, and it creates in the will a love without labour, spiritual and subtle. Now Christ says internally in the spirit by means of this flaming river: "Go forth by exercises according to the mode of these gifts and this coming." Thanks to the first river--that is to say, to a simple light, the memory is lifted up above the accidents of sense, and is established in the unity of spirit. Thanks to the second river-- that is to say, to the brightness spread abroad within, the intelligence and reason are enlightened, so as to recognise the diverse modes of the virtues and of exercises, and the mysteries of the Scriptures. Thanks to the third river--that is to say, to an inspired ardour, the sublime will is kindled into a more tranquil love, and adorned with greater riches. In this way a man becomes spiritually enlightened, for the grace of God abides, like a fountain in the unity of the spirit; and these rivers create in the faculties of the soul an effluence of all the virtues. And the fountain of grace always requires a reflux towards its source.

HOW CHRIST IS GIVEN TO ALL MEN IN THE SACRAMENT OF THE ALTAR

THERE is a special benefit which Christ left in the Holy Church, to all good people, in this supper of the great Paschal feast, when He was about to pass from His sufferings to His Father after having eaten the Paschal lamb with His disciples, and when the ancient law was accomplished. At the end of the supper, He wished to give them a special meal, as He had long desired to do. And this is why He wished to finish the ancient law and to inaugurate the new law. He took bread in His sacred hands, and consecrated His holy body, and then His holy blood, and gave them to all His disciples, and left them to all the just, for their eternal good.

This gift and this special food rejoice and adorn all the great festivals and all the banquets in heaven and on earth. In this gift Christ gives Himself to us in three manners; He gives us His flesh and blood and His bodily life, glorified and full of joys and griefs. And He gives us His spirit with its highest faculties, and full of glory, of gifts, of truths and justifications. And He gives us His personality with the divine light which lifts up His spirit and all enlightened spirits, even to the sublime and joyous unity.

Now Christ wishes us to remember Him, whenever we consecrate, offer, and receive His body. Now observe how we should remember Him. We shall observe and consider how Christ bends towards us in loving affection, in great desire, in loving joy, and by flowing into our bodily nature. For He gives us that which He received from our humanity--that is to say, His flesh and blood and bodily nature. We shall contemplate this precious body pierced and wounded with love, by reason of His faithfulness to us. It is by it that we are adorned and nourished in the lower part of our human nature. He gives us also, in this sublime gift of the sacrament, His spirit full of glory, and the richest gifts of the virtues, and ineffable marvels of charity and nobleness.

It is by this that we are nourished, adorned, and illuminated in the unity of our spirit and in our higher faculties, thanks to the indwelling of Christ with all His riches. He gives us also in the sacrament of the altar His sublime personality in incomprehensible light. And thanks to this, we are united to the Father, and so we reach our inheritance of divinity in eternal bliss. If a man meditate rightly on this, he will meet Christ in the same manner in which Christ comes to him. He will raise himself up to receive Christ, with all his faculties and in eager joy. It is not possible for our joy to be too great, for our nature receives His nature--that is to say the glorified humanity of Christ, full of joyfulness and full of merits. This is why I would that man, at the reception of this sacrament, should melt away with desire, joy, and pleasure, for he is receiving the fairest, the most gracious, the most lovable of the children of men, and is united to Him. In this union and in this joy great benefits often come to men, and many mysterious and marvellous secrets of divine treasures are manifested and disclosed. When a man meditates, at this reception, on the martyrdom and sufferings of the precious body of Christ, whom he is receiving, he enters sometimes into so loving a devotion and so great a compassion, that he desires to be nailed with Christ to the cross, and to shed his heart's blood for the honour of Christ. And he presses himself to the wounds and open heart of Christ His Saviour. In these exercises revelations and great benefits have often come to men.

ON THE UNITY OF THE DIVINE NATURE IN THE TRINITY OF

PERSONS

THE sublime and superessential unity of the Divine nature, in which the Father and the Son possess their nature in the unity of the Holy Spirit, above the conception and comprehension of all our faculties, in the bare essence of our spirit, surpasses in this sublime calm all the creatures of created light. This sublime unity of the Divine nature is living and fruitful, for, from this same unity, the eternal Word is born from the Father without interruption. And by this birth the Father knows the Son, and all things in the Son. And the Son knows the Father, and all things in the Father, for their nature is simple. From this reciprocal vision of the Father and the Son in an eternal clearness, flow forth an eternal satisfaction and unfathomable love, which is the Holy Spirit. And by the Holy Spirit and the eternal Wisdom God inclines towards every creature severally, and loads every one of them with gifts and kindles it with love, according to its nobility and according to the state wherein it is constituted and elected though its virtues and the eternal foresight of God. And it is by this that all just spirits, in heaven and on earth, are united in virtue and justice.

HOW GOD MOVES AND POSSESSES THE SOUL, NATURALLY AND SUPERNATURALLY

NOW be attentive: I am about to give you an example on this subject. God has made the upper heaven a pure and simple clearness encircling and enveloping all the heavens; and all the material world which God has created for it is the exterior abode and kingdom of God and His saints, full of glory and eternal joys. Now the heaven being an unmixed clearness, there is there neither time, nor state, nor temptation, nor change, for it is unchangeably fixed above all things. The sphere which approaches most nearly to it is called the primum mobile. All movement, by the power of God, emanates from the supreme heaven. This is the movement which carries with it the motions of the firmament and all the planets. It is by this same initial movement that all the creatures live and grow, according to their order. Now understand that the essence of the soul is like a spiritual kingdom of God, full of Divine clearness, surpassing all our faculties, unless these faculties are not transformed in a simple fashion, of which I do not wish to speak now. See; in this essence of the soul in which God reigns, the unity of our spirit is like the primum mobile; for in this unity the spirit is moved from above, by the power of God, naturally and supernaturally; for by ourselves we have nothing either in or above nature. And this motion of God, when it is supernatural, is the first and chief cause of all our virtue. And by this motion of God the seven gifts of the Holy Spirit are granted to certain enlightened men, like the seven planets which illuminate all the lives of men. This is how God possesses the essential unity of our spirit, as His Kingdom.

ON THE ESSENTIAL MEETING WITH GOD, WITHOUT INTERMEDIARY

NOW attend carefully. The unity of our spirit has two modes, one essential and the other active. You should know that the spirit, according to its essential existence, receives the coming of Christ in its bare nature, without intermediary and without interruption. For this essence and life which we are in God, in our eternal image, and which we have in ourselves, according to essential existence, are without intermediary and inseparable. This is why the spirit receives, in its highest and most intimate part, in its bare nature, the impression of its eternal image, and the divine brightness without interruption, and it is an eternal dwelling of God, which He occupies by a perpetual inhabitation, and which He visits always with a new coming, and a new effulgence from His eternal birth. For where He comes He is, and where He is He comes. And where He has never been, He will never come, for there is in Him neither accident nor change, and everything, where He is, is in Him, for He never goes out of Himself. And this is why the spirit possesses God essentially in its bare nature, and God the spirit, for the spirit lives in God, and God in the spirit. And it is capable, in its highest part, of receiving the brightness of God, and all that God may grant it, without intermediary. And by the brightness of its eternal image, which shines essentially and personally in it, the spirit is plunged, as regards the highest part of its vitality, in the divine essence; and there enters into possession of its eternal bliss, and flowing out again by the eternal birth of the Son is placed in its created essence by the free will of the Holy Trinity, And here it is like the image of the sublime Trinity and Unity for which it is created. And in its created nature, it takes the impression of its eternal image without interruption, like an immaculate mirror in which every impression abides, and which renews the likeness in itself without interruption. This essential unity of our spirit in God, exists not in itself, but abides in God and flows out from God, and is immanent in God and returns to God, as to its eternal cause. It never separates itself from God, for this unity is a fact of bare nature, and if nature separated itself from God it would fall into nothingness. And this unity is above time and conditions, and works always without interruption according to the mode of God. This is the nobleness which we have naturally according to the essential unity of our spirit, where it is united naturally to God.

This makes us neither saints nor blessed, for all men have it in them, the bad as well as the good; but it is the first cause of all holiness and bliss; and this is the meeting and unity of God in our spirit, in our base nature.

HOW MAN IS LIKE GOD BY GRACE, AND UNLIKE HIM BY MORTAL SIN

NOW examine this thought with care, for if you understand well what I wish to say to you, and what I have already said, you will understand all the divine truth which a creature can apprehend at present, and even things far more sublime. In the second mode, our spirit keeps itself actively in this same unity, and subsists by itself as in its personal created essence. This is the foundation and origin of the supreme faculties, and this is the beginning and end of all the works of a created nature, accomplished according to the mode of the creatures, both in nature and above nature.

Nevertheless this unity does not operate as unity; but all the faculties of the soul have their power entirely in their foundation--that is to say, in the unity of the spirit, where it resides in its personal essence. In this unity the spirit must always be like unto God, by grace and virtue, or unlike Him by mortal sin; for man is made in the likeness of God, which he must understand in the sense of grace; for grace is a deiform light which shines through us and makes us like unto God; and without this light we cannot be united supernaturally to God, even though we can never lose the image of God, nor our natural unity in Him. If we lose this likeness--that is to say, grace, we are damned. And this is why, so soon as God finds in us something which is capable of receiving His grace, He wishes to enliven us by His goodness, and to make us like unto Himself by His gifts. And this happens whenever we turn towards Him with full purpose; for at the same moment Christ comes to us and in us, with and without intermediary--that is to say, by the virtues and above all the virtues. And He impresses His image and likeness upon us--that is to say, Himself and all His gifts, and He relieves us from sin and makes us like unto Himself.

By the same operation in which God relieves us from sin, and makes us like Him and free in charity, the spirit is plunged in joyous love. And here take place a meeting and a union, which are without intermediaries and supernatural, and wherein resides our supreme blessedness. Although all that He gives by love and pure goodness is natural to God, yet to us it is accidental and supernatural, according to our mode, since formerly we were strangers and unlike, and only subsequently have become like God and obtained union with Him.

ON THE SUPREME DEGREE OF THE INTERIOR LIFE

NOW understand. This incomprehensible light transforms and penetrates the joyous inclination of our spirit. In this light, the spirit is plunged in joyous repose; for this repose is without mode and without bottom, and we can only know it by itself--that is to say, by repose. For if we could know it and conceive it, it would fall into mode and measure, and so would not be able to satisfy us, and repose would become an eternal restlessness. And this is why the simple, loving, complete inclination of our spirit forms in us a joyous love, and joyous love is without bottom. And the abyss of God calls to abyss; so it is with all those whose spirits are united to God in joyous love. This calling is an irruption from His essential brightness; and this essential brightness in the embrace of His bottomless love, causes us to lose ourselves and escape from ourselves, in the lonely darkness of God. And thus united, without intermediary, to the spirit of God, we can meet God by God, and possess unchangeably, with Him and in Him, our eternal blessedness.

ON THE FIRST MODE OF THIS HIGHEST MEETING

THE most interior life is practised in three ways. Sometimes the interior man operates, above all activity and all virtue, by simple introspection in joyous love. And here he meets God without intermediary. And from the unity of God a simple light shines in him, and this light shows him darkness, nakedness, and nothingness. He is enveloped in darkness, and falls into the absence of mode as one who loses his way. He loses, in nakedness, the power of observing and distinguishing all things, and he is transformed and penetrated by a simple brightness. He loses, in nothingness, all his works, for he is overcome in the work of the unlimited love of God; and in the joyous inclination of his spirit he triumphs in God and becomes one spirit with Him. This is the first mode, which is inactive; for it empties a man of all things, and lifts him up above works and virtues.

ON THE SECOND MODE

THERE are moments when the interior man turns desirously and actively towards God, to pay Him homage, and to offer up and annihilate, in the love of God, his being and all that he can give. And here he meets God, through an intermediary. This intermediary is the gift of wisdom, which is the foundation and source of all the virtues, and excites the just to virtues in proportion to their love; and sometimes it touches and inflames the interior man with love so violently, that all the gifts of God, and all that God can give without giving Himself, seem to him too little and do not satisfy him, but only increase his impatience. For he has at the bottom of his being an interior perception or sensation, wherein all the virtues begin and end, and wherein he offers to God all the virtues, and wherein love lives. And thus the hunger and thirst of love become so great, that he is reduced to nothingness, and then touched anew, as it were for the first time, by the irradiation of God. Thus in living he dies and in dying he lives again. This is the second mode, and it is more useful and more glorious than the first; for none can enter into the repose that is above action unless he has first actively loved love. And this is why none will be inactive, who is master of himself and who is able to practise love.

ON THE THIRD MODE

FROM these two kinds is born the third, which is an interior life according to righteousness. Now understand. God comes to us without interruption, with and. without intermediary, He requires of us action and joy, in such a way that action may not hinder joy, nor joy action, but that each may help the other. This is why the interior man possesses his life in these two modes, repose and work. And in each of them he is entire and undivided; for he is entirely in God, in his joyous repose, and he is entirely in himself, in his active love; and God warns him that He requires him to renew continually his repose and his work. The righteousness of the spirit wishes to pay, every hour, what God requires of us, and this is why, at every irradiation of God, the spirit turns inwards, actively and joyously, and so is renewed in all the virtues, and plunged more deeply in joyous love. For God at every gift gives Himself with all His gifts, and the spirit whenever it turns inwards, gives itself with all its works. The spirit is united to God, and transferred without interruption into repose. The man is hungry, for he sees the nourishment of angels and the food of heaven. He works actively in love, for he sees his repose. He is a pilgrim, and he sees his country. He fights, in love, for victory, for he sees his crown. Consolation, peace, joy, beauty, and riches, and all that can rejoice the heart, are shown to the reason illuminated by God, in spiritual similitudes and without measure. And by this vision, at the touch of God, love remains active. For this just man has built up, in the spirit, a true life, which will last eternally, but after this life it will be transformed into a more sublime state. Thus the man is just, and he goes towards God by interior love in eternal work, and he goes in God by joyous inclination, in eternal repose. And he abides in God, and yet he goes out towards all the creatures, in common love, in the virtues, and in the works of justice. This is the supreme summit of the inner life.

Note.--Here follow in Ruysbroek's treatise four chapters of warnings against the errors of Quietism, such as were exemplified in his time by many of the Brethren of the Free Spirit and similar sects.

BOOK III

THE THREE CONDITIONS BY WHICH WE MAY ATTAIN TO THE CONTEMPLATIVE LIFE

THE interior lover of God, who possesses God in joyous repose, and possesses himself in the unity of active love, and possesses all his life in the virtues, enters into the contemplative life, thanks to these three points and to the secret manifestation of God; yes, it is the internal and devout lover, whom God will choose freely and lift him up even to a superessential contemplation in divine light and according to the mode of God. This contemplation places us in a purity and brightness above all intelligence, for it is a singular ornament and a celestial crown, and at last the eternal recompense of all the virtues and of all life. And none can arrive there by knowledge or subtlety, nor by any exercise; but he whom God wills to unite to His own Spirit and to illuminate by Himself, can contemplate God, and none other can. To such an one the heavenly Father says, in the secret and submerged part of the spirit: "See, the Bridegroom cometh, go forth to meet Him."

I wish to analyse and explain these words, in their relation to superessential contemplation, which is the basis of all holiness and of the perfect life. Very few men attain to this divine contemplation, by reason of our incapacity, and the mystery of the light in which contemplation takes place. And this is why no one, by his own knowledge or by any subtle examination, will understand these ideas. For all words, and all that can be learned and understood according to the mode of the creatures, are strangers to the truth which I speak of, and far below it. But he who is united to God, and illuminated in this truth, can comprehend the truth by itself. For to conceive and understand God above all similitudes, as He is in Himself, is to be God in God, without intermediary and without any difference which might prove an obstacle. This is why I desire that every man who does not understand this, nor experience it in the joyous unity of his spirit, may not be wounded by my words, for what I say is true. And this is why he who wishes to understand this, must be dead to himself and alive to God, and he will turn his face to the eternal light, at the bottom of his spirit, where the hidden truth is manifested without intermediary. For the heavenly Father wishes that we should be seeing; for He is the Father of Light, and this is why He says eternally, without interruption and without intermediary, one abysmal word and no other. In this word He proffers Himself and all things. The word is: "See." And it is the going forth and the birth of the Son of the eternal light, in whom we see and recognise all our blessedness.

HOW A MAN OUGHT TO EXERCISE HIMSELF, IN ORDER TO RECEIVE THE ETERNAL LIGHT AND TO CONTEMPLATE GOD

IN order that the spirit may contemplate God by God, without intermediary, in this Divine light, three things are necessary. First, the man must be well governed externally in all the virtues, and without obstacles within, and as free from all external works as if he did them not; for if he is troubled within by any act of virtue, he has images, and so long as they remain in him he cannot contemplate. In the second place, he must adhere internally to God, by the combination of intention and of love, like a burning fire, which can never more be extinguished. At the moment when he feels himself in this state, he can contemplate. In the third place, he should be lost in an absence of mode, and in a darkness, in which all contemplatives wander joyously, and can never find themselves again according to the mode of the creatures. In the abyss of this darkness, where the loving spirit is dead to itself, begin the manifestation of God and of eternal life. For in this darkness is born and shines an incomprehensible light, which is the Son of God, in whom we see eternal life. And in this light we become seeing; and this Divine light is given in the simple vision of the spirit, in which the spirit receives the clearness which is God Himself, without intermediary, and becomes without interruption this clearness which it receives. See; this dark clearness, in which we contemplate all that we desire, while the spirit is passive,--this clearness is so great than the loving contemplative, in the depth where he reposes, sees and experiences nothing save an incomprehensible light, and according to the simple nudity which envelopes all things, he sees and apprehends the same light by which he sees, and nothing else. This is the first condition of becoming seeing in the Divine light. Happy are the eyes which thus see, for they have eternal life.

HOW THE ETERNAL BIRTH OF GOD IS RENEWED WITHOUT INTERRUPTION IN NOBLENESS OF SPIRIT

WHEN we have thus become seeing, we can contemplate in joy the eternal coming of the Bridegroom, and this is the second point on which I wish to speak. What is then this coming of the Bridegroom which is eternal? It is a new birth and a new illumination without interruption; for the foundation out of which the clearness shines, and which is the clearness itself, is living and fruitful; and this is why the manifestation of the eternal light is renewed without interruption, in the most secret part of the spirit. See; every creaturely work, and every exercise of virtue must here submit themselves, for God works alone in the highest part of the spirit. There is nought here but an eternal contemplation and fixity of light, by light, and in light. And the coming of the Bridegroom is so swift that He comes always, and is immanent with His unfathomable riches, and comes back ever anew, in person, with such new splendours that He seems never to have come before. For His coming consists in an eternal Now, transcending time, and He is always received with new desire and new joy. The delights and joy which this Bridegroom brings at His coming are without bottom and without limits, for they are Himself. This is why the eyes of the spirit, by which the lover contemplates the Bridegroom, are open so wide that they will never more be shut. For the contemplation and fixity of the spirit remain eternal in the hidden manifestation of God. And the contemplation of the spirit is so widely opened, while waiting for the coming of the Bridegroom, that the spirit itself acquires the amplitude of that which it comprehends. And in this way, God is seen and comprehended by God, in which all our salvation and blessedness consists. This is the second manner in which we receive, without interruption in our spirit, the eternal coming of our Bridegroom.

ON THE ETERNAL GOING FORTH WHICH WE POSSESS IN THE BIRTH OF THE SON

NOW the Spirit of God saith, in the secret depths of our spirit: "Go forth," in an eternal contemplation and joy, according to the mode of God. All the wealth which is in God naturally, we possess in Him by love; and God possesses it in us, by His boundless Love, which is the Holy Spirit. For in this love all is tasted that can be desired. And this is why, thanks to this love, we are dead to ourselves, and have gone forth in loving liquefaction or immersion, in the absence of mode and in darkness. There the spirit, enveloped by the Holy Trinity, is eternally immanent in the superessential unity, in repose and in joy. And in this same unity, according to the mode of generation, the Father is in the Son, and the Son in the Father, and every creature in them both. And this is above the distinction of Persons, for here we understand by reason the fatherhood and sonship in the lively fruitfulness of nature.

Here is born and begins an eternal going forth, and an eternal work without beginning, for there is here a beginning without beginning. For by means of the eternal birth of the Son, the Word of the Father, all creatures have gone forth eternally, before they were created in time, and God has considered and recognised them distinctly in Himself, in lively reason, and in distinction from Himself: but not in another mode, for all that is in God is God. This eternal going forth and this eternal life, which we have and are eternally in God, without ourselves, is the cause of our created essence in time. And our created essence is immanent in the eternal essence, and this eternal life, which we have and are in the eternal wisdom of God, is like unto God; for they have an eternal immanence, without distinction, in the divine essence. And they have an eternal effluence by the birth of the Son, in a difference with distinction, according to the eternal reason. And thanks to these two things, a man is in this way like unto God, that he recognises himself and reflects on himself without interruption, in this resemblance, according to essence and according to the Persons. For though here there is still distinction and difference, according to reason, this resemblance is nevertheless one with the very image of the Holy Trinity, which is the wisdom of God, and wherein God contemplates Himself and all things in an eternal Now, without before or after. In simple vision He regards Himself as He regards all things. And this is the image and likeness of God, and our image and likeness, for in it God and all things are reflected. In this divine image, all the creatures, without themselves, have an eternal life, as in their eternal model, and the Holy Trinity has made us in this eternal image and likeness. And this is why God wishes that we should go out from ourselves, in this eternal light, and that we should pursue this image, which is our true life, supernaturally, and possess it with Him actively and joyously, in eternal blessedness.

For we know well that the bosom of the Father is our foundation and origin, wherein we begin our life and our being. And from our true foundation--that is to say, from the Father and from all that lives in Him, beams forth an eternal radiance, which is the birth of the Son. In this radiance, the Father manifests Himself, and all that lives in Himself, to Himself; for all that He is, and all that He has, He gives to the Son, except the prerogative of fatherhood, which resides in Himself. And this is why all that lives in the Father hidden in the Unity, lives also in the Son, and flows forth in His manifestation; but the simple foundation of our eternal image remains always without mode in the darkness. But the boundless radiance which shines out thence manifests and reflects in the mode the mystery of God. And all men who are raised above their creatureliness into a contemplative life, are united to this divine splendour. And they are this splendour itself, and they see, experience, and find, thanks to this divine radiance, that they are this same simple foundation, according to their uncreated essence, from which shines forth, in the divine mode, this immeasurable radiance, which, according to simplicity of essence, remains eternally within, and without mode. This is why interior men and contemplatives will go forth, according to the mode of contemplation, above distinction and above their created essence, by means of an eternal intuition. Thanks to this inborn light, they are transformed, and are united to this same light by which they see and which they see. In this manner contemplatives pursue the eternal image, after which they are made, and contemplate God and all things without distinction, by a pure vision in divine brightness. This is the most sublime and the most useful contemplation which we can attain in this life; for in this contemplation a man remains the best and freest master of himself, and at each loving introversion, above all that we can comprehend, he can advance in the sublimities of life, for he remains free and master of himself, in unity and in the virtues. And this contemplation in the divine light maintains him above all inwardness, above all virtue, above all merit, for it is the crown and recompense towards which we are striving, and which we already have and possess in this mode, for the contemplative life is a celestial life. But if we shall be drawn up out of this exile and this misery, we shall be, according to our created nature, more susceptible of this radiance, and then the glory of God would shine through us better and more sublimely. This is the mode above all modes, according to which we go forth in a divine contemplation and in an eternal stability, and according to which we are transformed and reformed in the divine radiance. This going forth of the contemplative is also loving; for by joyous love he surpasses his created essence, and finds and tastes the riches and delights which are God, and which He causes to flow without interruption into the most secret part of the spirit, into the place where he is like the sublimity of God.

ON THE DIVINE MEETING, WHICH TAKES PLACE IN THE MOST SECRET PART OF OUR SPIRIT

WHEN the interior man and contemplative has thus pursued his eternal image, and possessed in this purity the bosom of the Father by the Son, he is illuminated by the divine truth, and receives anew at each instant the eternal birth; and he goes forth according to the mode of light, in a divine contemplation. And here arises the fourth and last point--that is to say, the loving meeting, in which before all else resides our eternal blessedness.

You know that our heavenly Father, like a living foundation, is actively inclined towards His Son, as towards His own eternal wisdom. And this same wisdom, and all that lives therein, is actively inclined in the Father--that is to say, in the foundation whence it proceeds. And in this meeting arises the Third Person, between the Father and the Son, and this is the Holy Spirit, their mutual love, which is united to them both in the same nature. And He envelopes and penetrates, actively and joyously, the Father and the Son and all that lives in them with such riches and such joy, that all the creatures must be silent thereupon eternally, for the incomprehensible marvel of this love surpasses eternally the intelligence of all the creatures. But where we comprehend and taste this amazement, without being amazed, there the spirit is above itself, and one with the Spirit of God, and it tastes and sees, without measure, like God, the riches which He is Himself in the unity of the living foundation, where He possesses Himself according to the unity of His uncreated essence.

Now this delightful meeting is without interruption actively renewed in us, according to the mode of God, for the Father gives Himself in the Son, and the Son in the Father, in an eternal gratification and a loving embrace, and this is renewed at every hour in the ties of love; for even as the Father without interruption contemplates anew all things in the birth of His Son, so all things are beloved anew, by the Father and the Son, through the influence of the Holy Spirit. And this is the eternal meeting of the Father and the Son, in which we are lovingly wrapped by the Holy Spirit in eternal love.

Now this active meeting and this loving embrace are, in their foundation, joyous and without mode, for God's infinite absence of mode is so obscure and so destitute of mode, that it envelopes in itself every divine mode and every work, and the individuality of the Persons, in the rich envelopment of essential unity, and forms a divine rejoicing in the abyss of the unnameable. And here there is a joyous and outflowing immersion in the essential nakedness, where all the divine names and all the modes, and all divine reason, reflected in the mirror of the divine truth, fall into simple ineffability, in the absence of mode and of reason. For in this boundless abyss of simplicity, all things are enveloped in joyous blessedness, and the abyss remains itself uncomprehended save by the essential unity. Before this essential unity, the Persons must give way, and all that lives in God. For here is nought but an eternal rest, in a joyous envelopment of loving immersion, and this is the essence, without mode, which all interior spirits have chosen above all other things. It is the dark silence in which all lovers are lost. But if we could prepare ourselves thus for the virtues, we should unclothe ourselves, so to speak, from life, and should float on the wide expanses of this divine sea, and created things would no longer have power to touch us.

May we be able to possess, rejoicing, the essential unity, and clearly to contemplate the Unity in Trinity; and may the divine love, which rejects no suppliant, grant us this. Amen.

THEOLOGIA GERMANICA

SIN AND SELFISHNESS

SIN is nothing else but the turning away of the creature from the unchangeable Good to the changeable; from the perfect to the imperfect, and most often to itself. And when the creature claims for its own anything good, such as substance, life, knowledge, or power, as if it were that, or possessed it, or as if that proceeded from itself, it goeth astray. What else did the devil do, and what was his error and fall, except that he claimed for himself to be something, and that something was his and was due to him? This claim of his-- this "I, me, and mine," were his error and his fall. And so it is to this day. For what else did Adam do? It is said that Adam was lost, or fell, because he ate the apple. I say, it was because he claimed something for his own, because of his "I, me, and mine." If he had eaten seven apples, and yet never claimed anything for his own, he would not have fallen: but as soon as he called something his own, he fell, and he would have fallen, though he had never touched an apple. I have fallen a hundred times more often and more grievously than Adam; and for his fall all mankind could not make amends. How then shall my fall be amended? It must be healed even as Adam's fall was healed. And how, and by whom, was that healing wrought? Man could not do it without God, and God could not do it without man. Therefore God took upon Himself human nature; He was made man, and man was made God. Thus was the healing effected. So also must my fall be healed. I cannot do the work without God, and He may not or will not do it without me. If it is to be done, God must be made man in me also; God must take into Himself all that is in me, both within and without, so that there may be nothing in me which strives against God or hinders His work. Now if God took to Himself all men who are or ever lived in the world, and was made man in them, and they were deified in Him, and this work were not accomplished in me, my fall and my error would never be healed unless this were accomplished in me also. And in this bringing back and healing I can and shall do nothing of myself; I shall simply commit myself to God, so that He alone may do and work all things in me, and that I may suffer Him, and all His work, and His divine will. And because I will not do this, but consider myself to be mine own, and "I, me, and mine," and the like, God is impeded, and cannot do His work in me alone and without let or hindrance; this is why my fall and error remain unhealed. All comes of my claiming something for my own. ii., iii.

THE TWO EYES

We should remember the saying that the soul of Christ had two eyes, a right eye and a left eye. In the beginning, when the soul of Christ was created, she fixed her right eye upon eternity and the Godhead, and remained in the full beholding and fruition of the Divine essence and eternal perfection; and thus remained unmoved by all the accidents and labours, the suffering, anguish, and pain, that befell the outer man. But with the left eye she looked upon the creation, and beheld all things that are therein, and observed how the creatures differ from each other, how they are better or worse, nobler or baser; and after this manner was the outer man of Christ ordered. Thus the inner man of Christ, according to the right eye of His soul, stood in the full exercise of His Divine nature, in perfect blessedness, joy, and eternal peace. But the outer man and the left eye of the soul of Christ stood with Him in perfect suffering, in all His tribulations, afflictions and labours; in such a way that the inner or right eye remained unmoved, unimpeded and untouched by all the labour, suffering, woe, and misery that happened to the outer man. It has been said that when Jesus was bound to the pillar and scourged, and when He hung on the cross, according to the outer man, the inner man, a soul according to the right eye, stood in as full possession of Divine joy and blessedness as it did after the ascension, or as it does now. Even so His outer man, or soul according to the left eye, was never impeded, disturbed, or troubled by the inward eye in its contemplation of the outward things which pertained to it. The created soul of man has also two eyes. The one is the power of looking into eternity, the other the power of looking into time and the creatures, of perceiving how they differ from each other, of giving sustenance and other things necessary to the body, and ordering and ruling it for the best. But these two eyes of the soul cannot both perform their office at once; if the soul would look with the right eye into eternity, the left eye must be shut, and must cease to work: it must be as if it were dead. For if the left eye is discharging its office towards outward things-- if it is holding conversation with time and the creatures--then the right eye must be impeded in its working, which is contemplation. Therefore, he who would have one must let the other go; for no man can serve two masters. vii.

A FORETASTE OF ETERNAL LIFE

Some have asked whether it is possible for the soul, while it is still in the body, to reach so great a height as to gaze into eternity, and receive a foretaste of eternal life and blessedness. This is commonly denied; and in a sense the denial is true. For indeed it cannot come about, so long as the soul is occupied with the body, and the things which minister to the body and belong to it, and to time and created things, and is disturbed and troubled and distracted by them. For the soul that would mount to such a state, must be quite pure, entirely stripped and bare of all images; it must be wholly separate from all creatures, and above all from itself. Many think that this is impossible in this present life. But St Dionysius claims that it is possible, as we find from his words in his letter to Timothy, where he says: "In order to behold the hidden things of God, thou shalt forsake sense and the things of the flesh, and all that can be perceived by the senses, and all that reason can bring forth by her own power, and all things created and uncreated which reason can know and comprehend, and thou shalt stand upon an utter abandonment of thyself, as if thou knewest none of those things which I have mentioned, and thou shalt enter into union with Him who is, and who is above all existence and knowledge." If he did not think this to be possible in this present time, why did he teach it and urge it upon us in this present time? But you ought to know that a master has said, about this passage of St Dionysius, that it is possible, and may come to a man so often that he may become accustomed to it, and be able to gaze into eternity whenever he will. And a single one of these glances is better, worthier, higher, and more pleasing to God than all that the creature can do as a creature. He who has attained to it asks for nothing more, for he has found the kingdom of heaven and eternal life here on earth. viii.

DESCENT INTO HELL

Even as the soul of Christ had to descend into hell, before it ascended into heaven, so must the soul of man. And mark how this comes to pass. When a man truly perceives and considers who and what he is, and finds himself wholly base and wicked, and unworthy of all the consolation and kindness that he ever received, either from God or from the creatures, he falls into such a profound abasement and contempt for himself, that he thinks himself unworthy to walk upon the earth; he feels that he deserves that all creatures should rise against him and avenge their Maker upon him with punishments and torments; nay, even that were too good for him. And therefore he will not and dare not desire any consolation or release, either from God or any creature; he is willing to be unconsoled and unreleased, and he does not lament for his condemnation and punishment, for they are right and just, and in accordance with God's will. Nothing grieves him but his own guilt and wickedness; for that is not right, and is contrary to God's will: for this reason he is heavy and troubled. This is the meaning of true repentance for sin. And the man who in this life enters into this hell, enters afterwards into the kingdom of heaven, and has a foretaste of it which exceeds all the delights and happiness which he has ever had, or could have, from the things of time. But while a man is in this hell, no one can comfort him, neither God, nor the creatures. Of this condition it has been written, "Let me die, let me perish! I live without hope; from within and from without I am condemned, let no man pray for my deliverance." Now God has not forsaken a man, while he is in this hell, but He is laying His hand upon him, that he may desire nothing but the eternal Good only, and may discover that this is so noble and exceedingly good, that its blessedness cannot be searched out nor expressed, comfort and joy, peace, rest, and satisfaction. When, therefore, the man cares for and seeks and desires the eternal Good and nought beside, and seeks not himself, nor his own things, but the glory of God only, he is made to partake of every kind of joy, blessedness, peace, rest, and comfort, and from that time forward is in the kingdom of God.

This hell and this heaven are two good safe ways for a man in this present life, and he is happy who truly finds them. For this hell shall pass away, but this heaven shall abide for evermore. Let a man also observe, that when he is in this hell, nothing can console him; and he cannot believe that he shall ever be delivered or comforted. But when he is in heaven, nothing can disturb him: he believes that no one will ever be able to offend or trouble him again, though it is indeed possible that he may again be troubled and left unconsoled.

This heaven and hell come upon a man in such a way, that he knows not whence they come; and he can do nothing himself towards making them either come or depart. He can neither give them to himself, nor take them away from himself, neither bring them nor drive them away; even as it is written, "The wind bloweth where it listeth, and thou hearest the sound thereof, but canst not tell whence it cometh or whither it goeth." And when a man is in either of these two states, all is well with him, and he is as safe in hell as in heaven. And while a man is in the world, it is possible for him to pass many times from the one state into the other--even within a day and night, and without any motion of his own. But when a man is in neither of these two states, he holds intercourse with the creatures, and is carried this way and that, and knows not what manner of man he is. A man should therefore never forget either of these states, but carry the memory of them in his heart. xi.

THE THREE STAGES

Be well assured that none can be illuminated, unless he be first cleansed, purified, or stripped. Also none can be united to God unless he be first illuminated. There are therefore three stages--first, the purification; secondly, the illumination; and thirdly, the union. The purification belongs to those who are beginning or repenting. It is effected in three ways; by repentance and sorrow for sin, by full confession, and by hearty amendment. The illumination belongs to those who are growing, and it also is effected in three ways; by the renunciation of sin, by the practice of virtue and good works, and by willing endurance of all trials and temptations. The union belongs to those who are perfect, and this also is effected in three ways; by pureness and singleness of heart, by love, and by the contemplation of God, the Creator of all things. xiv.

THE LIFE OF CHRIST

We ought truly to know and believe that no life is so noble, or good, or pleasing to God, as the life of Christ. And yet it is to nature and selfishness the most bitter of all lives. For to nature, and selfishness, and the Me, a life of careless freedom is the sweetest and pleasantest, but it is not the best; indeed, in some men it may be the worst. But the life of Christ, though it be the bitterest of all, should be preferred above all. And hereby ye shall know this. There is an inward sight which is able to perceive the one true good, how that it is neither this nor that, but that it is that of which St Paul says: "When that which is perfect is come, then that which is in part shall be done away." By this he signifies that what is whole and perfect excels all the parts, and that all which is imperfect, and in part, is as nothing compared to what is perfect. In like manner, all knowledge of the parts is swallowed up when the whole is known. And where the good is known, it cannot fail to be desired and loved so greatly, that all other love, with which a man has loved himself, and other things, vanishes away. Moreover, that inward sight perceives what is best and noblest in all things, and loves it in the one true good, and for the sake of the true good alone. Where this inward sight exists, a man perceives truly that the life of Christ is the best and noblest life, and that it is therefore to be chosen above all others; and therefore he willingly accepts and endures it, without hesitation or complaining, whether it is pleasing or displeasing to nature and other men, and whether he himself likes or dislikes it, and finds it sweet or bitter. Therefore, whenever this perfect and true good is known, the life of Christ must be followed, until the decease of the body. If any man vainly deems otherwise, he is deceived, and if any man says otherwise, he tells a lie; and in whatever man the life of Christ is not, he will never know the true good or the eternal truth.

But let no one imagine that we can attain to this true light and perfect knowledge, and to the life of Christ, by much questioning, or by listening to others, or by reading and study, or by ability and deep learning. For so long as a man is occupied with anything which is this or that, whether it be himself or any other creature; or does anything, or forms plans, or opinions, or objects, he comes not to the life of Christ. Christ Himself declared as much, for He said: "If any man will come after Me, let him deny himself, and take up his cross, and follow Me." "And if any man hate not his father and mother, and wife and children, and brethren and sisters, yea and his own life also, he cannot be my disciple." He means this: "He who does not give up and abandon everything can never know My eternal truth, nor attain to My life." And even if this had not been declared to us, the truth itself proclaims it, for so verily it is. But as long as a man holds fast to the rudiments and fragments of this world, and above all to himself, and is conversant with them, and sets great store by them, he is deceived and blinded, and perceives what is good only in so far as is convenient and agreeable to himself and profitable to his own objects.

Since then the life of Christ is in all ways most bitter to nature and the self and the Me--for in the true life of Christ nature and the self and the Me must be abandoned and lost and suffered to die completely--therefore in all of us nature has a horror of it, and deems it evil and unjust and foolish; and she strives after such a life as shall be most agreeable and pleasant to ourselves; and says, and believes too in her blindness, that such a life is the best of all. Now nothing is so agreeable and pleasant to nature as a free and careless manner of life. To this therefore she clings, and takes enjoyment in herself and her powers, and thinks only of her own peace and comfort. And this is especially likely to happen, when a man has high natural gifts of reason, for reason mounts up in its own light and by its own power, till at last it comes to think itself the true eternal light, and gives itself out to be such; and it is thus deceived in itself, and deceives others at the same time, people who know no better and are prone to be so deceived. xviii.-xx.

UNION WITH GOD

In what does union with God consist? It means that we should be indeed purely, simply, and wholly at one with the one eternal Will of God, or altogether without will, so that the created will should flow out into the eternal Will and be swallowed up and lost in it, so that the eternal Will alone should do and leave undone in us. Now observe what may be of use to us in attaining this object. Religious exercises cannot do this, nor words, nor works, nor any creature or work done by a creature. We must therefore give up and renounce all things, suffering them to be what they are, and enter into union with God. Yet the outward things must be; and sleeping and waking, walking and standing still, speaking and being silent, must go on as long as we live.

But when this union truly comes to pass and is established, the inner man henceforth stands immoveable in this union; as for the outer man, God allows him to be moved hither and thither, from this to that, among things which are necessary and right. So the outer man says sincerely, "I have no wish to be or not to be, to live or die, to know or be ignorant, to do or leave undone; I am ready for all that is to be or ought to be, and obedient to whatever I have to do or suffer." Thus the outer man has no purpose except to do what in him lies to further the eternal Will. As for the inner man, it is truly perceived that he shall stand immoveable, though the outer man must needs be moved. And if the inner man has any explanation of the actions of the outer man, he says only that such things as are ordained by the eternal Will must be and ought to be. It is thus when God Himself dwells in a man; as we plainly see in the case of Christ. Moreover, where there is this union, which is the outflow of the Divine light and dwells in its beams, there is no spiritual pride nor boldness of spirit, but unbounded humility and a lowly broken heart; there is also an honest and blameless walk, justice, peace, contentment, and every virtue. Where these are not, there is no true union. For even as neither this thing nor that can bring about or further this union, so nothing can spoil or hinder it, except the man himself with his self-will, which does him this great injury. Be well assured of this. xxvii., xxviii.

THE FALSE LIGHT

Now I must tell you what the False Light is, and what belongs to it. All that is contrary to the true light belongs to the false. It belongs of necessity to the true light that it never seeks to deceive, nor consents that anyone should be injured or deceived; and it cannot be deceived itself. But the false light both deceives others, and is deceived itself. Even as God deceives no man, and wills not that any should be deceived, so it is with His true light. The true light is God or Divine, but the false light is nature or natural. It belongeth to God, that He is neither this nor that, and that He requires nothing in the man whom He has made to be partaker in the Divine nature, except goodness as goodness and for the sake of goodness. This is the token of the true light. But it belongs to the creature, and to nature, to be something, this or that, and to intend and seek something, this or that, and not simply what is good without asking Why. And as God and the true light are without all self-will, selfishness, and self-Seeking, so the "I, Me, and Mine" belong to the false light, which in everything seeks itself and its own ends, and not goodness for the sake of goodness. This is the character of the natural or carnal man in each of us. Now observe how it first comes to be deceived. It does not desire or choose goodness for its own sake, but desires and chooses itself and its own ends rather than the highest good; and this is an error and the first deception. Secondly, it fancies itself to be God, when it is nothing but nature. And because it feigns itself to be God, it takes to itself what belongs to God; and not that which belongs to God when He is made man, or when He dwells in a Godlike man; but that which belongs to God as He is in eternity without the creature. God, they say, and say truly, needs nothing, is free, exempt from toil, apart by Himself, above all things: He is unchangeable, immoveable, and whatever He does is well done. "so will I be," says the false light. "The more like one is to God, the better one is; I therefore will be like God and will be God, and will sit and stand at His right hand." This is what Lucifer the Evil Spirit also said. Now God in eternity is without contradiction, suffering, and grief, and nothing can injure or grieve Him. But with God as He is made man it is otherwise. The false light thinks itself to be above all works, words, customs, laws, and order, and above the life which Christ led in the body which He possessed in His human nature. It also claims to be unmoved by any works of the creatures; it cares not whether they be good or bad, for God or against Him; it keeps itself aloof from all things, and deems it fitting that all creatures should serve it. Further, it says that it has risen beyond the life of Christ according to the flesh, and that outward things can no longer touch or pain it, even as it was with Christ after the Resurrection. Many other strange and false notions it cherishes. Moreover, this false light says that it has risen above conscience and the sense of sin, and that whatever it does is right. One of the so-called "Free Spirits" even said that if he had killed ten men, he would have as little sense of guilt as if he had killed a dog. This false light, in so far as it fancies itself to be God, is Lucifer, the Evil Spirit; but in so far as it makes of no account the life of Christ, it is Antichrist. It says, indeed, that Christ was without sense of sin, and that therefore we should be so. We may reply that Satan also is without sense of sin, and is none the better for that. What is a sense of sin? It is when we perceive that man has turned away from God in his will, and that this is man's fault, not God's, for God is guiltless of sin. Now, who knows himself to be free from sin, save Christ only? Scarce will any other affirm this. So he who is without sense of sin is either Christ or the Evil Spirit. But where the true light is, there is a true and just life such as God loves. And if a man's life is not perfect, as was that of Christ, still it is modelled and built on His, and His life is loved, together with modesty, order, and the other virtues, and all self-will, the "I, Me, and Mine," is lost; nothing is devised or sought for except goodness for its own sake. But where the false light is, men no longer regard the life of Christ and the virtues, but they seek and purpose what is convenient and pleasant to nature. From this arises a false liberty, whereby men become regardless of everything. For the true light is the seed of God, and bringeth forth the fruits of God; but the false light is the seed of the Devil, and where it is sown, the fruits of the Devil, nay the very Devil himself, spring up. xl.

LIGHT AND LOVE

It may be asked, What is it like to be a partaker of the Divine nature, or a Godlike man? The answer is, that he who is steeped in, or illuminated by, the eternal and Divine Light, and kindled or consumed by the eternal and Divine Love, is a Godlike man and a partaker of the Divine nature. But this light or knowledge is of no avail without love. You may understand this if you remember that a man who knows very well the difference between virtue and wickedness, but does not love virtue, is not virtuous, in that he obeys vice. But he who loves virtue follows after it, and his love makes him an enemy to wickedness, so that he will not perform any wicked act and hates wickedness in others; and he loves virtue so that he would not leave any virtue unperformed even if he had the choice, not for the sake of reward, but from love of virtue. To such a man virtue brings its own reward, and he is content with it, and would part with it for no riches. Such a man is already virtuous, or in the way to become so. And the truly virtuous man would not cease to be so to gain the whole world. He would rather die miserably. The case of justice is the same. Many men know well what is just and unjust, but yet neither are nor ever will be just men. For they love not justice, and therefore practise wickedness and injustice. If a man loved justice, he would do no unjust deed; he would feel so great abhorrence and anger against injustice whenever he saw it that he would be willing to do and suffer anything in order to put an end to injustice, and that men might be made just. He would rather die than commit an injustice, and all for love of justice. To him, justice brings her own reward, she rewards him with herself, and so the just man would rather die a thousand deaths than live as an unjust man. The same may be said of truth. A man may know very well what is truth or a lie, but if he loves not the truth, he is not a true man. If, however, he loves it, it is with truth as with justice. And of justice Isaiah speaks in the fifth chapter: "Woe unto them that call evil good, and good evil, that put darkness for light, and light for darkness; that put bitter for sweet, and sweet for bitter." Thus we may understand that knowledge and light avail nothing without love. We see the truth of this in the case of the Evil One. He perceives and knows good and evil, right and wrong: but since he has no love for the good that he sees, he becomes not good. It is true indeed that Love must be led and instructed by knowledge, but if knowledge is not followed by Love, it will be of no avail. So also with God and Divine things. Although a man know much about God and Divine things, and even dream that he sees and understands what God Himself is, yet if he have not Love, he will never become like God or a partaker of the Divine nature. But if Love be added to his knowledge, he cannot help cleaving to God, and forsaking all that is not God or from God, and hating it and fighting with it, and finding it a cross and burden. And this Love so unites a man to God, that he can never again be separated from Him. xli.

PARADISE

What is Paradise? All things that are. For all things are good and pleasant, and may therefore fitly be called Paradise. It is also said, that Paradise is an outer court of heaven. In the same way, this world is truly an outer court of the eternal, or of eternity; and this is specially true of any temporal things or creatures which manifest the Eternal or remind us of eternity; for the creatures are a guide and path to God and eternity. Thus the world is an outer court of eternity, and therefore it may well be called a Paradise, for so indeed it is. And in this Paradise all things are lawful except one tree and its fruit. That is to say, of all things that exist, nothing is forbidden or contrary to God, except one thing only. That one thing is self-will, or to will otherwise than as the eternal Will would have it. Remember this. For God says to Adam (that is, to every man) "Whatever thou art, or doest, or leavest undone, or whatever happens, is lawful if it be done for the sake of and according to My will, and not according to thy will. But all that is done from thy will is contrary to the eternal Will." Not that everything which is so done is in itself contrary to the eternal Will, but in so far as it is done from a different will, or otherwise than from the Eternal and Divine Will. l.

WILL AND SELF-WILL

Some may ask: "If this tree, Self-Will, is so contrary to God and to the eternal will, why did God create it, and place it in Paradise?" We may answer: a man who is truly humble and enlightened does not ask God to reveal His secrets to him, or enquire why God does this or that, or prevents or allows this or that; he only desires to know how he may please God, and become as nothing in himself, having no will of his own, and that the eternal will may live in him, and possess him wholly, unhampered by any other will, and how what is due may be paid to the Eternal Will, by him and through him. But there is another answer to this question. For we may say: the most noble and gracious gift that is bestowed on any creature is the Reason and the Will. These two are so intimately connected that the one cannot be anywhere without the other. If it were not for these two gifts, there would be no reasonable creatures, but only brutes and brutality; and this would be a great loss, for God would then never receive His due, or behold Himself and His attributes exhibited in action; a thing which ought to be, and is, necessary to perfection. Now Perception and Reason are conferred together with will, in order that they may teach the will and also themselves, that neither perception nor will is of itself, or to itself, nor ought to seek or obey itself. Nor must they turn themselves to their own profit, nor use themselves for their own ends; for they belong to Him from whom they proceed, and they shall submit to Him, and flow back to Him, and become nothing in themselves--that is, in their selfhood.

But now you must consider more in detail something concerning the will. There is an Eternal Will, which is a first principle and substance in God, apart from all works and all externalisation; and the same will is in man, or the creature, willing and bringing to pass certain things. For it pertains to the will, to will something. For what else does it exist? It would be a vain thing if it had no work to do, and this it cannot have without the creature. And so there must needs be creatures, and God will have them, in order that by their means the will may be exercised, and may work, though in God it must be without work. Therefore the will in the creature, which we call the created will, is as truly God's as the eternal will, and is not from the creature.

And since God cannot exercise His will, in working and effecting changes, without the creature, He is pleased to do so in and with the creature. Therefore the will is not given to be exercised by the creature, but by God alone, who has the right to carry into effect His own will by the will which is in man, but yet is God's will. And in any man or creature, in whom it should be thus, purely and simply, the will of that man or creature would be exercised not by the man but by God, and thus it would not be self-will, and the man would only will as God wills; for God Himself, and not man, would be moving the will. Thus the will would be united with the Eternal Will, and would flow into it; although the man would retain his sense of liking and disliking, pleasure and pain. But nothing is complained of, except what is contrary to God. And there is no rejoicing except in God alone, and in that which belongs to Him. And as with the will, so is it with all the other faculties of man; they are all of God and not of man. And when the will is wholly given up to God, the other faculties will certainly be given up too; and God will have what is due to Him.

No one may call that which is free his own, and he who makes it his own, doeth injustice. Now in all the sphere of freedom nothing is so free as the will; and he who makes it his own, and allows it not to remain in its excellent freedom, and free nobleness, and free exercise, does it a great injustice. This is what is done by the devil, and Adam, and all their followers. But he who leaves the will in its noble freedom does right; and this is what Christ, and all who follow Him, do. And he who deprives the will of its noble freedom, and makes it his own, must necessarily be oppressed with cares and discontent, and disquietude, and every kind of misery, and this will be his lot throughout time and eternity. But he who leaves the will in its freedom has contentment and peace and rest and blessedness, through time and eternity. Where there is a man whose will is not enslaved, he is free indeed, and in bondage to no man. He is one of those to whom Christ said: "The truth shall make you free"; and He adds immediately afterwards: "If the Son shall make you free, ye shall be free indeed."

Moreover, observe that whenever the will chooses unhindered whatever it will, it always and in all cases chooses what is noblest and best, and hates whatever is not noble and good, and regards it as an offence. And the more free and unhampered the will is, the more it is grieved by evil, by injustice, by iniquity, and all manner of sin. We see this in Christ, whose will was the purest and freest and the least brought into bondage of any man's who ever lived. So was the human nature of Christ the most free and pure of all creatures; and yet He felt the deepest distress, pain, and wrath at sin that any creature ever felt. But when men claim freedom for themselves, in such a way as to feel no sorrow or anger at sin, and all that is contrary to God, and say that we must take no notice of anything, and care for nothing, but be, in this life, what Christ was after the resurrection, and so forth, this is not the true and Divine freedom that springs from the true and Divine light, but a natural, unrighteous, false, deceiving freedom, which springs from the natural, false, deceitful light.

If there were no self-will, there would be no proprietorship. There is no proprietorship in heaven; and this is why contentment, peace, and blessedness are there. If anyone in heaven were so bold as to call anything his own, he would immediately be cast out into hell, and become an evil spirit. But in hell everyone will have self-will, and therefore in hell is every kind of wretchedness and misery. And so it is also on earth. But if anyone in hell could rid himself of his self-will and call nothing his own, he would pass out of hell into heaven. And if a man, while here on earth, could be entirely rid of self-will and proprietorship, and stand up free and at liberty in the true light of God, and continue therein, he would be sure to inherit the kingdom of heaven. For he who has anything, or who desires to have anything of his own, is a slave; and he who has nothing of his own, nor desires to have anything, is free and at liberty, and is in bondage to no man. li.

UNION THROUGH CHRIST

Observe now how the Father draws men to Christ. When something of the perfect good is revealed and made manifest within the human soul, as it were in a sudden flash, the soul conceives a desire to draw near to the perfect goodness, and to unite herself with the Father. And the more strongly she longs and desires, the more is revealed to her; and the more is revealed to her, the more she is drawn to the Father, and the more is her desire kindled. So the soul is drawn and kindled into an union with the eternal goodness. And this is the drawing of the Father; and so the soul is taught by Him who draws her to Himself, that she cannot become united with Him unless she can come to Him by means of the life of Christ. liii.

[1]In his Introduction to the "Imitation of Christ," in this series.

[2]e.g. she distinguishes, as Eckhart does, between God and the Godhead.

[3]The "three propositions" of Amalric are--1. "Deus est omnia." 2. Every Christian, as a con-dition of salvation, must believe that he is a member of Christ. 3. To those who are in charity no sin is imputed.

[4]Preger is probably wrong in identifying him with a "brother Eckhart," Prior of Frankfort, who about 1320 was delated to the head of the Order as suspectus de malis familiaritatibus, words which can only mean "keeping bad company" in a moral sense, not "con-sorting with heretics," as Preger suggests. Eckhart's character, so far as we know, was never assailed, even by his enemies, and it is therefore probable that "brother Eckhart" was a different person.

[5]I have abridged the bull considerably, but have included all the main accusations.

[6]See pages 13, 16.

[7]See pages 14, 15.

[8]See page 1.

[9]This is an obscure point in Eckhart's philosophy, too technical to be discussed here; but Eckhart's doctrine of God is certainly more orthodox and less pantheistic than those of 'Dionysius' and Scotus Erigena.

[10]Cf. St Augustine, In Joann. Ev. Tract. xxxix. 10: praeteritum et futurum invenio in omni motu rerum: in veritate quae manet praeteritum et futurum

non invenio, sed solum praesens.

[11]This doctrine is fully explained by St. Augustine, Epist. 237, who follows Plotinus, Enn. vi. 4-6.

[12]This queer word occurs for the first time, I think, in Jerome's notes to the first chapter of Ezekiel. He writes the word in Greek, and explains it as that part of the soul which always opposes vices. The word is common in Bonaventura and other scholastic mystics, and is often misspelt synderesis.

[13]It must, however, be said that Preger is too ready to assume that the logical development of Eckhart's system away from Thomist scholasticism can be traced as a gradual process in his writings, the order of which is very uncertain. We are not justified in saying in a positive manner that Eckhart's philosophy passed through three phases, in the first of which the primacy is held by the will, in the second by the created reason, and in the third by the uncreated reason.

[14]See pages 14, 15.

[15]C.B. Upton: "Hibbert Lectures," p. 17.

[16]A.E. Taylor: "The Problem of Conduct," PP. 464-5.

[17]See pages 71-2.

[18]See pages 12-13.

[19]See, for example, Prof. W. James' "Varieties of Religions Experience," P. 400.

[20]Jacob Bšhme's experience is typical: "Suddenly did my spirit break through into the innermost birth or geniture of the Deity, and there was I embraced with love, as a bridegroom embraces his dearly beloved bride. But the greatness of the triumphing that was in the spirit I cannot express in speech or writing; nor can it be compared to anything but the resurrection of the dead to life. In this light my spirit suddenly saw through all; even in herbs and grass it knew God, who and what He is," etc. Dr Johnson was, no doubt, right in

thinking that "Jacob" would have been wiser, and "more like St Paul," if he had not attempted to utter the unutterable things which he saw.

[21]The extracts from the "Theologia Germanica" will show that this treatise represents a later and less paradoxical form of mystical thought than Eckhart's.

[22]The maxim, however, is much older than Suso.

[23]Royce: "The World and the Individual" vol. i. p. 193.

[24]So in the "Lignum Vitae" of Laurentius Justinianus we read: "Let self-will cease, and there will be no more hell."

[25] "The Inner Way," being thirty-six sermons by John Tauler. Translated by A.W. Hutton, M.A.

[26]On the psychology of ecstatic mysticism see Leuba, in the Revue Philosophique, July and November 1902.

[27] "Varieties of Religious Experience," p. 13.

[28]Maudsley: "Natural Causes and Supernatural Seemings," p. 256.

[29]See Leuba: "Tendances religieuses chez les mystiques chr 閨 iens" in Revue Philosophique, Nov. 1902.

[30] "Theologia Germanica," translated by Susanna Winkworth. Macmillan & Co., 1893.

[31] "Varieties of Religious Experience," 1902.

[32] "Personal Idealism," 1902.

[33] "Varieties of Religious Experience," p. 103.

[34] "In Tune with the Infinite," by R.W. Trine (Bell & Sons, 1902). Fifty-ninth thousand. The extract appears to be a quotation from another writer, but no reference is given.

[35]Compare Eckhart's saying that the eye with which I see God is the same as the eye with which He sees me.

[36] "In Tune with the Infinite," pp. 58, 119.

[37]The numbers refer to pages in Pfeiffer's edition.

[38]The numbers refer to the Sermons in Hamberger's edition of 1864.

[39]The reference is to 1 Peter iii. 8.

[40]The time would, I suppose, be about half-an-hour. Many other ecstatics have named this as the normal duration of trance.

[41]Or, "spoke the eternal Wisdom (= the Word of God) in his heart."

[42]John i. 3, 4. This punctuation, whereby the words "that which was made" are referred to the clause which follows, and not to that which precedes, is adopted by most of the Greek fathers, and is still maintained by some good commentators--e.g. Bishop Westcott.

[43]Ecclus. xxiv. 19.

[44]Ecclus. xl. 20.